Spelling Skills

Grade 5

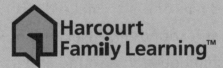

Harcourt
Family Learning™

© 2005 by Flash Kids
Adapted from *Steck-Vaughn Spelling: Linking Words to Meaning, Level 5*
by John R. Pescosolido
© 2002 by Harcourt Achieve
Licensed under special arrangement with Harcourt Achieve.

ISBN: 978-1-4114-0386-4

Please submit all inquiries to FlashKids@bn.com

Manufactured in Canada

Lot #:
17 19 21 20 18 16
07/15

Flash Kids
A Division of Barnes & Noble
122 Fifth Avenue
New York, NY 10011

Dear Parent,

As your child learns to read and write, he or she is bound to discover that the English language contains very many words, and that no single set of rules is used to spell all of these words. This can feel rather confusing and overwhelming for a young reader. But by completing the fun, straightforward activities in this workbook, your child will practice spelling the words that he or she is most likely to encounter in both classroom and everyday reading. To make the path to proper spelling even easier, each lesson presents fifth-grade words in lists grouped by vowel sound or related forms, like plurals, homophones, and compound words. This order will clearly show your child the different ways that similar sounds can be spelled.

Each of the 30 lessons begins by asking your child to say each word in the word list. This exercise helps him or her to make the connection between a word's appearance and what it sounds like. Next, he or she will sort the words, which teaches the relationship between a sound and its spelling patterns. Your child will then encounter a variety of activities that will strengthen his or her understanding of the meaning and use of each word. These include recognizing definitions, synonyms, and parts of speech, completing analogies, as well as using capitalization and punctuation. Be sure to have a children's or adult dictionary available, which your child will need to use for some of the exercises. Each lesson also features a short passage containing spelling and grammar mistakes that your child will proofread and correct, using the proofreading marks on page 7. Once he or she can recognize both correct and incorrect spellings, your child is ready for the next lesson!

Throughout this workbook are brief unit reviews to help reinforce knowledge of the words that have been learned in the lessons. Your child can use the answer key to check his or her work in the lessons and reviews. Also, take advantage of everyday opportunities to improve spelling skills. By asking your child to read stories or newspaper articles to you at home, or billboards and signs while traveling, you are showing your child how often he or she will encounter these words. You can also give your child extra practice in writing these correct spellings by having him or her write a shopping list or note to a family member.

Since learning to spell can be frustrating, your child may wish to use one or more of the spelling strategies on page 6 when he or she finds a word or group of words difficult to master. You can also encourage your child to use the following study steps to learn a word:

1. Say the word. What consonant sounds do you hear? What vowel sounds do you hear? How many syllables do you hear?

2. Look at the letters in the word. Think about how each sound is spelled. Find any spelling patterns or parts that you know. Close your eyes. Picture the word in your mind.

3. Spell the word aloud.

4. Write the word. Say each letter as you write it.

5. Check the spelling. If you did not spell the word correctly, use the study steps again.

With help from you and this workbook, your child is well on the way to excellent skills in spelling, reading, and writing!

table of contents

unit 5

unit 6

spelling strategies

What can you do when you aren't sure how to spell a word?

Say the word aloud. Make sure you say it correctly. Listen to the sounds in the word. Think about letters and patterns that might spell the sounds.

Look in the Spelling Table on page 141 to find common spellings for sounds in the word.

Think about related words. They may help you spell the word you're not sure of.

instruction—instruct

Guess the spelling of the word and check it in a dictionary.

Write the word in different ways. Compare the spellings and choose the one that looks correct.

tuch   toch   (touch)   tooch

Think about any spelling rules you know that can help you spell the word.

To form the plural of a singular word ending in a consonant and y, change the y to i and add -es.

Listen for a common word part, such as a prefix, a suffix, or an ending.

appoint<u>ment</u>

person<u>al</u>

Break the word into syllables and think about how each syllable might be spelled.

an-i-ma-tion

Create a memory clue to help you remember the spelling of the word.

<u>Cloth</u>ing is made of <u>cloth</u>.

Proofreading Marks

Mark	Meaning	Example
⬭	spell correctly	I ⬭liek⬭ dogs.
⊙	add period	They are my favorite kind of pet ⊙
?	add question mark	What kind of pet do you have ?
≡	capitalize	My dog's name is s̲cooter.
ℒ	take out	He is a great companion for me and my ~~my~~ family.
∧	add	We got Scooter when ∧he∧ was eight weeks old.
/	make lowercase	My Ⱥncle came over to take a look at him.
∼	trade places	He watched the puppy run (in around) circles.
⌄⌄	add quotation marks	⌄⌄Scooter! That's the perfect name! ⌄⌄ I said.
¶	indent paragraph	¶ I love my dog Scooter. He is the best pet I have ever had. Every morning he wakes me with a bark. Every night he sleeps with me.

Words with /ă/

act	sandwich	traffic	magic
chapter	rabbit	snack	rapid
plastic	laughter	calf	program
planet	crash	salad	aunt
factory	magnet	half	crack

Say and Listen

Say each spelling word. Listen for the /ă/ sound you hear in *act*.

Think and Sort

Look at the letters in each word. Think about how /ă/ is spelled. Spell each word aloud.

How many spelling patterns for /ă/ do you see?

1. Write the **eighteen** spelling words that have the *a* pattern, like *act*.

2. Write the **two** spelling words that have the *au* pattern, like *laughter*.

planet

1. a Words

_____   _____   _____
_____   _____   _____
_____   _____   _____
_____   _____   _____
_____   _____   _____
_____   _____   _____

2. au Words

_____   _____

Definitions

Write the spelling word for each definition.
Use a dictionary if you need to.

1. a heavenly body that circles the sun   _____
2. a place where things are made   _____
3. the movement of cars and trucks   _____
4. a young cow or bull   _____
5. a sound that shows amusement   _____
6. a ceremony or presentation   _____
7. a substance made from chemicals   _____

Analogies

An analogy states that two words go together in the same way as two others. Write the spelling word that completes each analogy.

8. *Perform* is to _____ as *exercise* is to *jog*.
9. *Big* is to *large* as *fast* is to _____.
10. A *third* is to *three* as _____ is to *two*.
11. *Bear* is to *honey* as *nail* is to _____.
12. *Feast* is to _____ as *mansion* is to *cottage*.
13. *Correct* is to *right* as *smash* is to _____.
14. *Hire* is to *employ* as *split* is to _____.
15. *Man* is to *woman* as *uncle* is to _____.
16. *Lettuce* is to _____ as *flour* is to *bread*.
17. *Kitty* is to *cat* as *bunny* is to _____.
18. *Room* is to *house* as _____ is to *book*.
19. *Artist* is to *art* as *magician* is to _____.

act	sandwich	traffic	magic
chapter	rabbit	snack	rapid
plastic	laughter	calf	program
planet	crash	salad	aunt
factory	magnet	half	crack

Proofreading

Proofread the e-mail message below. Use proofreading marks to correct five spelling mistakes, three capitalization mistakes, and two punctuation mistakes. See the chart on page 7 to learn how to use the proofreading marks.

Proofreading Marks

◯ spell correctly
＝ capitalize
⊙ add period

---

e-mail

New	Read	File	Delete	Sea

Hi, andy,

   This weekend I went skiing with my dad I was coming

down a hill at a rapud speed when a calf ran out in front of

me. I managed to avoid hitting it, but i tripped and landed

with a krash. Nothing was hurt but the egg salad sanwitch

I had brought along as a snak. it was squashed flat in

its plastic wrapper I burst into laugter at the sight! What did

you do this weekend? Let's talk later!

Bailey

Alphabetical Order

Words are listed in alphabetical order in a dictionary.
When two letters are the same, the next letter is used to alphabetize them.

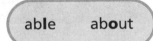 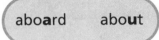

about   around   able   about   aboard   about

Write each group of words in alphabetical order.

1. traffic   half   rabbit   plastic

_____

_____

_____

_____

2. program   aunt   planet   act

_____

_____

_____

_____

3. chapter   calf   crack   factory

_____

_____

_____

_____

4. salad   sandwich   magic   magnet

_____

_____

_____

_____

5. loose   laughter   library   length

_____

_____

_____

_____

6. raw   raccoon   rabbit   rapid

_____

_____

_____

_____

Words with /ā/

paid	bakery	weight	remain	escape
raise	brain	delay	break	male
snake	weigh	scale	neighbor	container
complain	holiday	explain	parade	female

Say and Listen

Say each spelling word. Listen for the /ā/ sound you hear in *paid*.

weight

Think and Sort

Look at the letters in each word. Think about how /ā/ is spelled. Spell each word aloud.

How many spelling patterns for /ā/ do you see?

1. Write the **six** spelling words that have the *a-consonant-e* pattern, like *male*.
2. Write the **one** spelling word that has the *a* pattern.
3. Write the **nine** spelling words that have the *ai* or *ay* pattern, like *paid*.
4. Write the **three** spelling words that have the *eigh* pattern, like *weigh*.
5. Write the **one** spelling word that has the *ea* pattern.

1. a-consonant-e Words

_____ _____ _____

_____ _____ _____

2. a Word

_____

3. ai, ay Words

_____ _____ _____

_____ _____ _____

_____ _____ _____

4. eigh Words

_____ _____ _____

5. ea Word

_____

Clues

Write the spelling word for each clue.

1. This is a kind of reptile. _____

2. People use a scale to do this. _____

3. This word is the opposite of *fix*. _____

4. People do this to tell why. _____

5. This word is the opposite of *leave*. _____

6. A band might march in one of these. _____

7. A jar is one kind of this. _____

8. This word is the opposite of *lower*. _____

9. People may do this when they don't like something. _____

10. This is a special day. _____

Hink Pinks

Hink pinks are pairs of rhyming words that have a funny meaning.
Read each meaning. Write the spelling word that completes each hink pink.

11. a locomotive carrying geniuses _____ train

12. a hotel worker on pay day _____ maid

13. a light-colored weighing device pale _____

14. something that is very heavy great _____

15. a story told by a woman _____ tale

16. what is used to build a community garden _____ labor

17. plastic cakes and pies _____ fakery

18. a story about a man _____ tale

19. why the employees were paid late pay _____

paid	brain	scale	parade
raise	weigh	explain	escape
snake	holiday	remain	male
complain	weight	break	container
bakery	delay	neighbor	female

Proofreading

Proofread the journal entry below. Use proofreading marks to correct five spelling mistakes, three capitalization mistakes, and two punctuation mistakes.

Proofreading Marks

◯ spell correctly

☰ capitalize

⊙ add period

March 9

I found out today that our nayber, pete, has a

pet snake. he named the snake Toby Toby is a mayle

garter snake, and he has beautiful stripes on his

back. He sleeps in a cage that Pete made out of a

wooden apple contayner. He spends the rest of his

time watching Pete's pet mice. They look a little

nervous to me.

I like Toby, but I hope he will remane at Pete's

house He had better not excape and decide to visit

my house. having him next door is just fine with me!

Sentences

A sentence begins with a capital letter and ends with a punctuation mark.
A sentence that tells something ends with a period.

> I like chicken soup**.**

A sentence that asks a question ends with a question mark.

> Do you like chicken soup**?**

A sentence that shows strong feeling or surprise ends with an exclamation point.

> Don't spill the chicken soup**!**

The following sentences contain errors in capitalization and punctuation.
Write each sentence correctly.

1. our class planned a holiday vacation

_____

2. mr. Peterson bought fresh bread at the bakery

_____

3. watch out for that snake by your foot

_____

4. what did you do on your break from school

_____

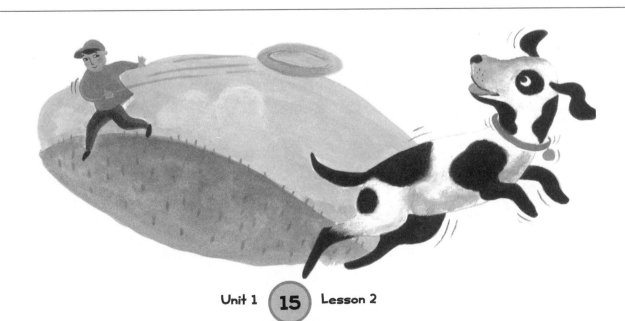

Words with /ĕ/

bench	healthy	thread	intend
invent	wealth	sentence	weather
self	instead	friendly	questions
measure	address	breath	pleasure
checkers	sweater	depth	treasure

Say and Listen

Say each spelling word. Listen for the /ĕ/ sound you hear in *bench*.

Think and Sort

sweater

Look at the letters in each word. Think about how /ĕ/ is spelled. Spell each word aloud.

How many spelling patterns for /ĕ/ do you see?

1. Write the **nine** spelling words that have the *e* pattern, like *bench*.

2. Write the **ten** spelling words that have the *ea* pattern, like *thread*.

3. Write the **one** spelling word that has the *ie* pattern.

1. e Words

_____   _____   _____

_____   _____   _____

_____   _____   _____

2. ea Words

_____   _____   _____

_____   _____   _____

_____   _____   _____

_____

3. ie Word

_____

Classifying

Write the spelling word that belongs in each group.

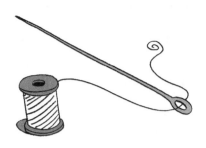

1. coat, jacket, _____

2. pins, needle, _____

3. name, phone number, _____

4. pirate, map, _____

5. width, height, _____

6. well, fit, _____

7. warm, kind, _____

8. statements, exclamations, _____

Rhymes

Write the spelling word that completes each sentence and
rhymes with the underlined word.

9. Mr. <u>Beckers</u> and I enjoy playing _____ together.

10. Did you _____ the distance to the hidden <u>treasure</u>?

11. I sat on the _____ to study my <u>French</u>.

12. Good <u>health</u> is better than all the _____ in the world.

13. <u>Heather</u> doesn't like rainy _____.

14. On cold mornings, <u>Seth</u> can see his _____.

15. The sick <u>elf</u> did not feel like her normal _____.

16. Maria and Jonas _____ to <u>send</u> letters to the editor.

17. Henry wants to _____ a lightweight <u>tent</u>.

18. Dave will go with us _____ of <u>Ted</u>.

19. It is impossible to <u>measure</u> my _____.

bench	healthy	thread	intend
invent	wealth	sentence	weather
self	instead	friendly	questions
measure	address	breath	pleasure
checkers	sweater	depth	treasure

Proofreading

Proofread the article below. Use proofreading marks to correct five spelling mistakes, two capitalization mistakes, and three missing words.

Proofreading Marks
◯ spell correctly
≡ capitalize
∧ add

All the Right Moves

A huge crowd was on hand for annual cheakers

tournament last weekend. because the wethar was bad,

the contest took place in the school gymnasium insted

of at the park. The mood was frendly as players took

their places and qestions were answered. Spectators

held their breath as they watched play after play. beth

Meadows was finally named champion. She will

compete in the state meet Memphis next month. The

runner-up was Ben Treasure, who also took home

trophy.

Dictionary Skills

Guide Words

Guide words are the two words in dark type at the top of each dictionary page. The first guide word is the first word on the page. The second guide word is the last word on the page.

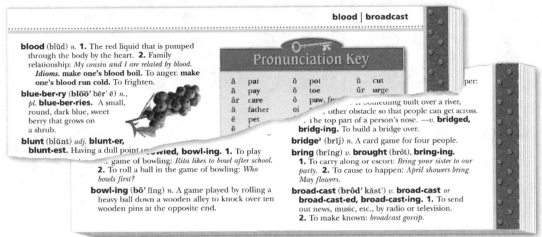

Write the following words in alphabetical order. Then look up each word in a dictionary and write the guide words for the page on which it appears.

bench   address   measure   intend   sentence   wealth

Word	Guide Words	
1. _____	_____	_____
2. _____	_____	_____
3. _____	_____	_____
4. _____	_____	_____
5. _____	_____	_____
6. _____	_____	_____

More Words with /ĕ/

else	century	extra	remember
pledge	selfish	petal	exercise
elephant	energy	desert	length
expert	metal	excellent	vegetable
metric	wreck	gentle	special

Say and Listen

Say each spelling word. Listen for the /ĕ/ sound.

Think and Sort

The /ĕ/ sound is spelled e in each of the spelling words. Some of the spelling words have one e. Others have more than one e, but only one is pronounced /ĕ/. Look at the letters in each word. Spell each word aloud.

elephant

1. Write the **nine** spelling words that have one *e*, like *century*.

2. Write the **eleven** spelling words that have more than one *e*. Circle the *e* that has the /ĕ/ sound, like *pl(e)dge*.

1. Words with One e

_____   _____   _____
_____   _____   _____
_____   _____   _____

2. Words with More Than One e

_____   _____   _____
_____   _____   _____
_____   _____   _____
_____   _____

Analogies

Write the spelling word that completes each analogy.

1. *Pineapple* is to *fruit* as *squash* is to _____.

2. *Wet* is to *dry* as *ocean* is to _____.

3. *Weak* is to *powerful* as _____ is to *generous*.

4. *Annoying* is to *irritating* as *wonderful* is to _____.

5. *Branch* is to *tree* as _____ is to *rose*.

6. *Construct* is to *build* as _____ is to *destroy*.

7. *Penny* is to *dollar* as *year* is to _____.

8. *Width* is to *wide* as _____ is to *long*.

9. *Recall* is to _____ as *border* is to *edge*.

10. *Oak* is to *wood* as *copper* is to _____.

Definitions

Write the spelling word for each definition.

11. relating to the system of weights and measures based on meters and grams _____

12. mild _____

13. more than what is usual or expected _____

14. besides; in addition _____

15. different from others _____

16. physical activity that improves the body _____

17. ability to do work _____

18. a serious promise _____

19. someone with special skill or knowledge _____

else	century	extra	remember
pledge	selfish	petal	exercise
elephant	energy	desert	length
expert	metal	excellent	vegetable
metric	wreck	gentle	special

Proofreading

Proofread the news article below. Use proofreading marks to correct five spelling mistakes, two punctuation mistakes, and three unnecessary words.

Proofreading Marks

◯ spell correctly
⊙ add period
℮ take out

Master of the Air

Anna Chung is is an expurt circus acrobat visiting

Cedar Rapids this month. In an interview for the Daily

News, Ms. Chung told us about her work

"I remeber to practice every day. I also get plenty

of of rest and exerize. If I didn't, I wouldn't have

the enerjy to give a an

excellant performance."

To see Chung in a

performance this

weekend, call 555-6262

Nouns

A noun is a word that names a person, a place, a thing, or an idea.
Proper nouns are capitalized. Common nouns are not.

Person	Place	Thing	Idea
teenager	desert	pumpkin	happiness
Cody	Utah	Lee Street	

Unscramble each sentence and write it correctly. Then circle the nouns.

1. drove desert week We the last through.

_____

2. the down swam wreck The to divers.

_____

3. Elephants Africa large are from animals.

_____

4. ran field length Andy the of the.

_____

5. vegetable Jill on ate plate every her.

_____

6. pen can't where I remember put and I paper my.

_____

7. globe to circle Explorers the seventeenth began century the in.

_____

Capitalized Words

October	December	Sunday	August	November
Monday	Thursday	May	July	September
June	March	January	Saturday	Friday
Tuesday	Wednesday	April	February	St.

Say and Listen

Say each spelling word. Listen for the vowel sounds.

Think and Sort

October

A **syllable** is a word part or a word with one vowel sound. *Thursday* has two syllables. *October* has three syllables.

Look at the letters in each word. Think about the number of syllables in the word. Spell each word aloud.

1. Write the **three** spelling words that have one syllable, like *March.*

2. Write the **nine** spelling words that have two syllables, like *A-pril.*

3. Write the **five** spelling words that have three syllables, like *Oc-to-ber.*

4. Write the **two** spelling words that have four syllables, like *Jan-u-ar-y.*

5. Write the **one** spelling word that is an abbreviation for *Street* and *Saint.*

---

1. One-syllable Words

_____   _____   _____

2. Two-syllable Words

_____   _____   _____

_____   _____   _____

_____   _____   _____

3. Three-syllable Words

_____   _____   _____

_____   _____

4. Four-syllable Words   **5.** Abbreviation

_____   _____   _____

Hink Pinks

Read each meaning. Write the spelling word that completes each hink pink.

1. a doorway to spring   _____ arch

2. a song sung in a summer month   _____ tune

3. a day in the fifth month   _____ day

4. to recall the first month of fall   remember _____

Clues

Write the spelling word for each clue.

5. the first day of the school week   _____

6. the day after Monday   _____

7. the day after Saturday   _____

8. a short way of writing *Street*   _____

9. the month in which many people celebrate the new year   _____

10. the last day of the school week   _____

11. the eleventh month of the year   _____

12. the day before Friday   _____

13. the month after September   _____

14. the fourth month of the year   _____

15. the day before Sunday   _____

16. the day that begins with *W*   _____

17. the shortest month of the year   _____

18. the last month of the year   _____

19. the month that is the middle of summer   _____

October	Thursday	January	February
Monday	March	April	November
June	Wednesday	August	September
Tuesday	Sunday	July	Friday
December	May	Saturday	St.

Proofreading

Proofread the letter below. Use proofreading marks to correct five spelling mistakes, three capitalization mistakes, and two punctuation mistakes.

Proofreading Marks
- ◯ spell correctly
- ≡ capitalize
- ⊙ add period

---

dear Grandma,

Thank you so much for the new flute! It sounds great

Every Wednesday I take lessons at mr. han's house on

Forest Ste. On Munday, Octobre 10, I give my first

recital. Our school band will play for the Veterans Day

parade on Teusday, Novumber 11 Will you come to hear

me play?

Love,

Jeremy

Using the Spelling Table

If you need to look up a word in a dictionary but aren't sure how to spell it, a spelling table can help. A spelling table lists common spellings for sounds. Suppose you are not sure how the first vowel sound in *August* is spelled. First, look in the table to find the pronunciation symbol for the sound. Then read the first spelling listed for /ô/, and look up *Agust* in a dictionary. Look for each spelling in the dictionary until you find the correct one.

Sound	Spellings	Example Words
/ô/	a au aw o ough o_e ou oa	already, autumn, raw, often, thought, score, court, roar

The following words contain boldfaced letters that represent sounds. Write each word correctly, using a dictionary and the Spelling Table on page 141.

1. rec**e**d _____

2. **a**lment _____

3. **e**sel _____

4. b**i**lt _____

5. myster**e** _____

6. l**a**ghter _____

7. l**oo**nar _____

8. **k**omet _____

9. cu**s**in _____

10. br**e**th _____

11. fr**e**ndly _____

12. bu**s**e _____

13. bri**j** _____

14. ri**l**ax _____

15. sk**e** _____

16. **g**ide _____

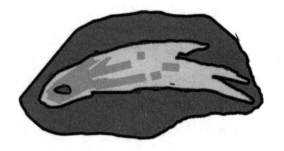

unit 1 Review
Lessons 1–5

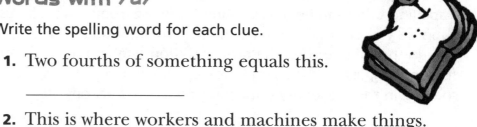

sandwich
factory
half
laughter

Words with /ă/

Write the spelling word for each clue.

1. Two fourths of something equals this.

_____

2. This is where workers and machines make things.

_____

3. This has meat between two slices of bread.

_____

4. When people respond to a funny joke, you hear this.

_____

escape
parade
bakery
holiday
container
neighbor
break

Words with /ā/

Write the spelling word for each definition.

5. a public event for a special occasion _____

6. a place where bread is sold _____

7. a person who lives nearby _____

8. a day such as Thanksgiving _____

9. to break loose or get away _____

10. a gap or an opening _____

11. a box, a jar, or a can used to hold something

_____

depth
wealth
breath
treasure
friendly

Words with /ĕ/

Write the spelling word that completes each analogy.

12. *Sociable* is to _____ as *bashful* is to *shy*.

13. *Brain* is to *thought* as *lung* is to

_____ .

Say and Listen

Say each spelling word. Listen for the vowel sounds.

Think and Sort

October

A **syllable** is a word part or a word with one vowel sound. *Thursday* has two syllables. *October* has three syllables.

Look at the letters in each word. Think about the number of syllables in the word. Spell each word aloud.

1. Write the **three** spelling words that have one syllable, like *March.*

2. Write the **nine** spelling words that have two syllables, like *A-pril.*

3. Write the **five** spelling words that have three syllables, like *Oc-to-ber.*

4. Write the **two** spelling words that have four syllables, like *Jan-u-ar-y.*

5. Write the **one** spelling word that is an abbreviation for *Street* and *Saint.*

---

1. One-syllable Words

_____   _____   _____

2. Two-syllable Words

_____   _____   _____

_____   _____   _____

_____   _____   _____

3. Three-syllable Words

_____   _____   _____

_____   _____

4. Four-syllable Words   **5.** Abbreviation

_____   _____   _____

Capitalized Words

October	December	Sunday	August	November
Monday	Thursday	May	July	September
June	March	January	Saturday	Friday
Tuesday	Wednesday	April	February	St.

Say and Listen

Say each spelling word. Listen for the vowel sounds.

Think and Sort

October

A **syllable** is a word part or a word with one vowel sound. *Thursday* has two syllables. *October* has three syllables.

Look at the letters in each word. Think about the number of syllables in the word. Spell each word aloud.

1. Write the **three** spelling words that have one syllable, like *March*.

2. Write the **nine** spelling words that have two syllables, like *A-pril*.

3. Write the **five** spelling words that have three syllables, like *Oc-to-ber*.

4. Write the **two** spelling words that have four syllables, like *Jan-u-ar-y*.

5. Write the **one** spelling word that is an abbreviation for *Street* and *Saint*.

1. One-syllable Words

_____   _____   _____

2. Two-syllable Words

_____   _____   _____

_____   _____   _____

_____   _____   _____

3. Three-syllable Words

_____   _____   _____

_____   _____

4. Four-syllable Words

5. Abbreviation

_____   _____

Hink Pinks

Read each meaning. Write the spelling word that completes each hink pink.

1. a doorway to spring _____ arch
2. a song sung in a summer month _____ tune
3. a day in the fifth month _____ day
4. to recall the first month of fall   remember _____

Clues

Write the spelling word for each clue.

5. the first day of the school week _____

6. the day after Monday _____

7. the day after Saturday _____

8. a short way of writing *Street* _____

9. the month in which many people celebrate the new year _____

10. the last day of the school week _____

11. the eleventh month of the year _____

12. the day before Friday _____

13. the month after September _____

14. the fourth month of the year _____

15. the day before Sunday _____

16. the day that begins with *W* _____

17. the shortest month of the year _____

18. the last month of the year _____

19. the month that is the middle of summer _____

October	Thursday	January	February
Monday	March	April	November
June	Wednesday	August	September
Tuesday	Sunday	July	Friday
December	May	Saturday	St.

Proofreading

Proofread the letter below. Use proofreading marks to correct five spelling mistakes, three capitalization mistakes, and two punctuation mistakes.

Proofreading Marks

◯ spell correctly

≡ capitalize

⊙ add period

dear Grandma,

Thank you so much for the new flute! It sounds great

Every Wednesday I take lessons at mr. han's house on

Forest Ste. On Munday, Octobre 10, I give my first

recital. Our school band will play for the Veterans Day

parade on Teusday, Novumber 11 Will you come to hear

me play?

Love,

Jeremy

October	Thursday	January	February
Monday	March	April	November
June	Wednesday	August	September
Tuesday	Sunday	July	Friday
December	May	Saturday	St.

Proofreading

Proofread the letter below. Use proofreading marks to correct five spelling mistakes, three capitalization mistakes, and two punctuation mistakes.

Proofreading Marks

⬭ spell correctly

☰ capitalize

⊙ add period

dear Grandma,

Thank you so much for the new flute! It sounds great

Every Wednesday I take lessons at mr. han's house on

Forest Ste. On Munday, Octobre 10, I give my first

recital. Our school band will play for the Veterans Day

parade on Teusday, Novumber 11 Will you come to hear

me play?

Love,

Jeremy

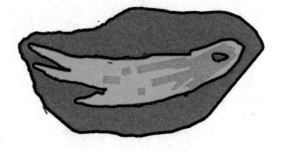

Dictionary Skills

Using the Spelling Table

If you need to look up a word in a dictionary but aren't sure how to spell it, a spelling table can help. A spelling table lists common spellings for sounds. Suppose you are not sure how the first vowel sound in *August* is spelled. First, look in the table to find the pronunciation symbol for the sound. Then read the first spelling listed for /ô/, and look up *Agust* in a dictionary. Look for each spelling in the dictionary until you find the correct one.

Sound	Spellings	Example Words
/ô/	a au aw o ough o_e ou oa	already, autumn, raw, often, thought, score, court, roar

The following words contain boldfaced letters that represent sounds. Write each word correctly, using a dictionary and the Spelling Table on page 141.

1. reced _____

2. aliment _____

3. esel _____

4. bilt _____

5. mystere _____

6. laghter _____

7. loonar _____

8. komet _____

9. cusin _____

10. breth _____

11. frendly _____

12. buse _____

13. brij _____

14. rilax _____

15. ske _____

16. gide _____

Dictionary Skills

Using the Spelling Table

If you need to look up a word in a dictionary but aren't sure how to spell it, a spelling table can help. A spelling table lists common spellings for sounds. Suppose you are not sure how the first vowel sound in *August* is spelled. First, look in the table to find the pronunciation symbol for the sound. Then read the first spelling listed for /ô/, and look up *Agust* in a dictionary. Look for each spelling in the dictionary until you find the correct one.

Sound	Spellings	Example Words
/ô/	a au aw o ough o_e ou oa	already, autumn, raw, often, thought, score, court, roar

The following words contain boldfaced letters that represent sounds. Write each word correctly, using a dictionary and the Spelling Table on page 141.

1. reced _____   **2.** alment _____

3. esel _____   **4.** bilt _____

5. mystere _____   **6.** laghter _____

7. loonar _____   **8.** komet _____

9. cusin _____   **10.** breth _____

11. frendly _____   **12.** buse _____

13. brij _____   **14.** rilax _____

15. ske _____   **16.** gide _____

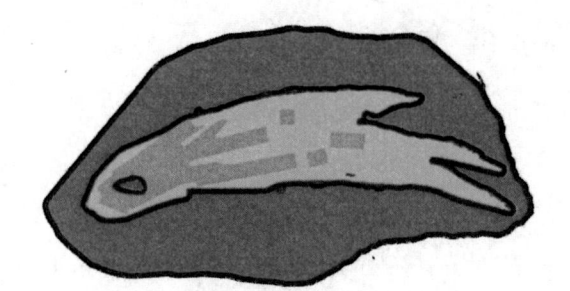

14. *Cookie* is to *jar* as _____ is to *chest*.

15. *Riches* is to _____ as *story* is to *tale*.

16. *Mountain* is to *ocean* as *height* is to _____.

LESSON 4

length
special
exercise
excellent
vegetable

More Words with /ĕ/

Write the spelling word that belongs in each group.

17. fruit, grain, _____

18. outstanding, wonderful, _____

19. width, height, _____

20. different, unique, _____

21. diet, rest, _____

LESSON 5

Tuesday
Saturday
January
February

Capitalized Words

Write the spelling word that completes each sentence.

22. The month of _____ is the shortest month of all.

23. Ling went to bed late Monday night and overslept _____ morning.

24. This weekend I have plans for _____, but not Sunday.

25. The new year for many people begins in the month of _____.

Words with /ē/

hobby	believe	compete	delivery
angry	evening	tardy	fancy
trapeze	athlete	merry	pretty
penalty	ugly	theme	liberty
empty	shady	busy	complete

Say and Listen

Say each spelling word. Listen for the /ē/ sound you hear in *hobby*.

Think and Sort

Look at the letters in each word. Think about how /ē/ is spelled. Spell each word aloud.

How many spelling patterns for /ē/ do you see?

athlete

1. Write the **thirteen** spelling words that have the *y* pattern, like *hobby*.

2. Write the **six** spelling words that have the *e*-consonant-*e* pattern, like *complete*.

3. Write the **one** spelling word that has the *ie* pattern.

1. y Words

_____   _____   _____

_____   _____   _____

_____   _____   _____

_____   _____   _____

_____

2. e-consonant-e Words

_____   _____   _____

_____   _____   _____

3. ie Word

_____

Classifying

Write the spelling word that belongs in each group.

1. swing, acrobat, _____
2. topic, subject, _____
3. displeasing, bad-looking, _____
4. vacant, hollow, _____
5. activity, interest, _____
6. think, suppose, _____
7. shadowy, dark, _____
8. morning, afternoon, _____
9. punishment, fine, _____
10. shipment, distribution, _____

Trading Places

Complete each sentence by writing the spelling word that
can take the place of the underlined word or words.

11. Our country has many symbols of _____. <u>freedom</u>
12. We sent some _____ flowers to our aunt. <u>lovely</u>
13. I was _____ that I fell down and skinned my knee! <u>furious</u>
14. Matthew was _____ this morning. <u>late</u>
15. Mom wore a _____ gown to the party. <u>elaborate</u>
16. The little man had a _____ laugh. <u>happy</u>
17. Tran leads a _____ life. <u>active</u>
18. This Canadian stamp makes my collection _____. <u>whole</u>
19. Ray will _____ in the race this Saturday. <u>take part</u>

hobby	believe	compete	delivery
angry	evening	tardy	fancy
trapeze	athlete	merry	pretty
penalty	ugly	theme	liberty
empty	shady	busy	complete

Proofreading

Proofread this paragraph from the back of a book.
Use proofreading marks to correct five spelling mistakes,
two capitalization mistakes, and two missing words.

Proofreading Marks

◯ spell correctly
≡ capitalize
∧ add

A Martian in the Library

It is friday evning. Daniel and Jasmine sit at a
table in the library. They are buzy doing a report
about life other planets. to their surprise,
Martian sits down in the emty seat next to them.
The Martian is not only uggly but very angry.
Readers won't beleive what happens next in this
intergalactic tale of loyalty, liberty, and
friendship written by the award-winning
author of fiction for young adults, Lisa Lowry.

Multiple Meanings

When you look up the meaning of a word in a sentence, you will often find that the word has several meanings. To know which one the writer intends, you must know the word's part of speech in the sentence. Then you can use other words in the sentence to decide on the correct meaning of the word.

> **com·plete** (kəm plēt′) *adj.* **1.** Whole: *a complete set of the encyclopedia.* **2.** Finished; ended: *My report is complete.* **3.** Fully equipped: *a new car complete with power steering.* —*v.* **com·plet·ed, com·plet·ing.** To finish.

> **emp·ty** (ĕmp′ tē) *adj.* **1.** Containing nothing. **2.** Without meaning: *empty promises.* —*v.* **emp·tied, emp·ty·ing, emp·ties.** To remove the contents of.

Use the dictionary entries above to write the part of speech and the definition for *empty* or *complete* in each of the following sentences.

	Part of Speech	Definition
1. Dad bought a sailboat **complete** with sails and motor.	_____	_____
2. My Saturday chore is to **empty** the trash cans.	_____	_____
3. I must **complete** my homework by six o'clock.	_____	_____
4. I wanted some juice, but the pitcher was **empty**.	_____	_____
5. Ashley has a **complete** set of the books you want.	_____	_____
6. The man's **empty** welcome made us feel uneasy.	_____	_____

More Words with /ē/

greet	pizza	weak	breathe
freeze	piano	speech	asleep
increase	peace	ski	defeat
reason	needle	steep	sheet
wheat	agree	degree	beneath

Say and Listen

Say each spelling word. Listen for the /ē/ sound.

Think and Sort

Look at the letters in each word. Think about how /ē/ is spelled. Spell each word aloud.

How many spelling patterns for /ē/ do you see?

pizza

1. Write the **eight** spelling words that have the *ea* pattern, like *weak*.

2. Write the **nine** spelling words that have the *ee* pattern, like *greet*.

3. Write the **three** spelling words that have the *i* pattern, like *pizza*.

---

1. ea Words

_____   _____   _____

_____   _____   _____

_____

2. ee Words

_____   _____   _____

_____   _____   _____

_____   _____   _____

3. i Words

_____   _____   _____

Classifying

Write the spelling word that belongs in each group.

1. thread, pins, _____

2. sled, skate, _____

3. inhale, exhale, _____

4. enlarge, grow, _____

5. beat, win, _____

6. under, below, _____

7. corn, oats, _____

8. spaghetti, ravioli, _____

9. ounce, watt, _____

10. guitar, violin, _____

11. pillow, blanket, _____

12. quiet, silence, _____

Rhymes

Write the spelling word that completes each sentence
and rhymes with the underlined word.

13. Each student had to give a _____.

14. After the race, the winner was too _____ to speak.

15. The raccoons creep up the _____ hill to our house.

16. Snow is the _____ I like the winter season.

17. When you meet them, _____ them with a smile.

18. Please give me my gloves before my hands _____.

19. The tired sheep were _____ in the meadow.

greet	pizza	weak	breathe
freeze	piano	speech	asleep
increase	peace	ski	defeat
reason	needle	steep	sheet
wheat	agree	degree	beneath

Proofreading

Proofread the paragraph below. Use proofreading marks to correct five spelling mistakes, three capitalization mistakes, and two unnecessary words.

Proofreading Marks

◯ spell correctly
= capitalize
ℓ take out

A Baker's Life

Uncle Al gets up early and is open for business when I go to school. Sometimes I stop in, and we eat hot doughnuts together. When i enter to his bakery and breeth in, lovely aromas greet me. that is one reazon why I am want to be a baker. I also like to help Uncle Al toss the wheet dough for pitza or roll it into balls for rolls. I enjoy taking baked cookies off the big cookie sheat, too. a baker's life is the life for me!

Predicates

Every sentence has two main parts, the complete subject and the complete predicate. The complete subject includes all the words that tell whom or what the sentence is about. The complete predicate includes all the words that tell what the subject does or is.

Complete Subject
The little gray kitten

Complete Predicate
followed me all the way to the fair.

Use the words in the boxes to complete each sentence below. Then circle the complete predicate.

ski   agree   freeze   greet

steep   defeat   speech

1. The team from Smallville is difficult to _____.

2. We will _____ down these snowy mountains every winter.

3. All the students listened to the principal's farewell _____.

4. That mountain is much too _____ to climb.

5. The pond behind our barn began to _____ at midnight.

6. We all _____ on the date for Maria's surprise party.

7. Ling can _____ him at the door.

Words with /ĭ/

wrist	guitar	expect	chimney
riddle	bridge	guilty	enough
since	disease	except	equipment
built	quit	quickly	relax
review	different	discuss	divide

Say and Listen

Say each spelling word. Listen for the /ĭ/ sound you hear in *wrist*.

Think and Sort

bridge

Look at the letters in each word. Think about how /ĭ/ is spelled. Spell each word aloud.

How many spelling patterns for /ĭ/ do you see?

1. Write the **eleven** spelling words that have the *i* pattern, like *wrist*.

2. Write the **five** spelling words that have the *e* pattern, like *expect*.

3. Write the **one** spelling word that has both the *i* and *e* patterns.

4. Write the **three** spelling words that have the *ui* pattern after a consonant other than *q*, like *built*.

1. i Words

_____   _____   _____

_____   _____   _____

_____   _____   _____

_____   _____

2. e Words

_____   _____   _____

_____   _____

3. i and e Word

_____

4. ui Words

_____   _____   _____

Analogies

Write the spelling word that completes each analogy.

1. *Under* is to *tunnel* as *over* is to _____.

2. *Ankle* is to *leg* as _____ is to *arm*.

3. *Add* is to *subtract* as *multiply* is to _____.

4. *Wrong* is to *right* as _____ is to *innocent*.

5. *Water* is to *faucet* as *smoke* is to _____.

6. *Stop* is to _____ as *start* is to *begin*.

7. *Walk* is to *slowly* as *run* is to _____.

8. *Same* is to *like* as _____ is to *unlike*.

9. *Jog* is to *exercise* as *nap* is to _____.

10. *Before* is to *preview* as *after* is to _____.

Clues

Write the spelling word for each clue.

11. You have this if you have as much as you need. _____

12. You did this if you made a house. _____

13. Baseball bats, balls, and gloves are this. _____

14. You play this by strumming its strings. _____

15. This kind of joke asks a question. _____

16. This is another word for *because*. _____

17. You do this when you think a thing will happen. _____

18. You do this when you talk with other people about something. _____

19. You might use this word instead of *but*. _____

wrist	guitar	expect	chimney
riddle	bridge	guilty	enough
since	disease	except	equipment
built	quit	quickly	relax
review	different	discuss	divide

Proofreading

Proofread the letter below. Use proofreading marks to correct five spelling mistakes, three capitalization mistakes, and two punctuation mistakes.

Proofreading Marks

◯ spell correctly
≡ capitalize
⊙ add period

14th Street SW

Calgary, AB

Canada T2T 3Y9

May 7, 2004

Dear Marty,

you asked how I learned to play the keyboard

It's been a year sinse I started lessons There are so

many diferent things to learn, and i wanted to learn

everything quikly. The best thing I learned is to relaax.

I just remember to take it slowly and never qwit.

Your friend,

ted

Capitalization

Capitalize the names of days and months.

> Sally was born on a **Friday** in **December**.

The following scrambled sentences contain errors in capitalization and spelling. Unscramble each sentence and write it correctly.

1. my april broke last I rist.

_____

2. our sinse february had We've trampoline.

_____

3. field discus june Let's go where our on trip in we'll.

_____

4. chimley september built Dad our a house new last on.

_____

5. and july expeck can really august weather We hot in.

_____

6. before to I tuesday our test riview need my notes on.

_____

7. theater saturday go diffrent We'll to move a next.

_____

More Words with /ĭ/

business	system	package	skill
chicken	mystery	arithmetic	film
message	picnic	kitchen	damage
village	sixth	garbage	pitch
insect	cottage	insist	timid

Say and Listen

Say each spelling word. Listen for the /ĭ/ sound.

Think and Sort

cottage

Look at the letters in each word. Think about how /ĭ/ is spelled. Spell each word aloud. How many spelling patterns for /ĭ/ do you see?

1. Write the **eleven** spelling words that have the *i* pattern, like *film*.

2. Write the **two** spelling words that have the *y* pattern, like *mystery*.

3. Write the **five** spelling words that have the *a* pattern, like *cottage*.

4. Write the **one** spelling word that has the *i* and *a* patterns.

5. Write the **one** spelling word that has the *u* pattern.

---

1. i Words

_____   _____   _____
_____   _____   _____
_____   _____   _____
_____

2. y Words

_____   _____

3. a Words

_____   _____   _____
_____   _____

4. i and a Word   **5. u Word**

_____   _____

Making Connections

Write the spelling word that relates to each person listed below.

1. a farmer _____

2. a baseball player _____

3. a movie director _____

4. a math teacher _____

5. a chef _____

6. a mail carrier _____

Definitions

Write the spelling word for each definition.
Use a dictionary if you need to.

7. a group of related things that make up a whole _____

8. a meal eaten outside _____

9. a small group of houses and businesses _____

10. trash _____

11. a small house _____

12. one of six equal parts _____

13. shy or lacking in self-confidence _____

14. news sent from one person to another _____

15. injury or harm _____

16. the ability to do something well _____

17. to take a stand or demand strongly _____

18. a small creature with wings and six legs _____

19. what a person does to earn a living _____

business	system	package	skill
chicken	mystery	arithmetic	film
message	picnic	kitchen	damage
village	sixth	garbage	pitch
insect	cottage	insist	timid

Proofreading

Proofread this paragraph. Use proofreading marks to correct five spelling mistakes, three capitalization mistakes, and two punctuation mistakes.

Proofreading Marks

◯ spell correctly
≡ capitalize
⊙ add period

Bees in our House!

We had bees in our kytchen, but not for long. My dad is good at catching them. he showed me how he does it. First, he lowers a glass carefully over the bee. Next, he slips a postcard under the glass Then, he takes the whole thing outside and lets the bee go. i tried to catch one of the bees in our kitchen, but I couldn't get the glass over it because the bee scared me A bee is not a timud insec. Last year I was stung near a garbige can at a picnec. Since then I've never cared much for picnics—or bees.

Commas

A series is a list of three or more items. The items can be single words or groups of words. A comma is used to separate the items in a series.

> Bill had a sandwich, a piece of pie, and a glass of milk.
> Then he gathered up his baseball glove, bat, and ball.

Write the following sentences correctly, adding commas where they are needed and correcting the misspelled words.

1. I need a pencil an eraser and some paper to do my arithmatick.

_____

2. Chikcen can be fried broiled or baked.

_____

3. We saw tulips roses and daisies outside the cottige.

_____

4. The villaje had a bakery a post office and a town hall.

_____

5. Lynn wanted to study history bizness and medicine.

_____

6. The timmid elephant was afraid of mice, snakes, and his own shadow!

_____

Plural Words

stories	speeches	penalties	neighbors	athletes
calves	wives	crashes	degrees	hobbies
parties	sandwiches	benches	wishes	vegetables
exercises	companies	branches	skis	businesses

Say and Listen

Say the spelling words. Notice the ending sounds and letters.

Think and Sort

sandwiches

A **plural** is a word that names more than one thing. A **base word** is a word to which suffixes, prefixes, and endings can be added. All of the spelling words are plurals. Most plurals are formed by adding -s to a base word. Other plurals are formed by adding -es.

The spelling of some base words changes when -es is added. A final y is often changed to i. An f is often changed to v.

Look at the spelling words. Think about how each plural is formed. Spell each word aloud.

1. Write the **six** spelling words formed by adding -s to the base word, like *skis*.

2. Write the **seven** -es spelling words that have no changes in the base word, like *branches*.

3. Write the **seven** -es spelling words that have changes in the spelling of the base word, like *wives*.

1. -s Plurals

_____ _____ _____
_____ _____ _____

2. -es Plurals with No Base Word Changes

_____ _____ _____
_____ _____ _____
_____

3. -es Plurals with Base Word Changes

_____ _____ _____
_____ _____ _____
_____

Clues

Write the spelling word for each clue.

1. Corn and spinach are kinds of these. _____

2. You can use these to slide over snow. _____

3. You make these with bread and a filling. _____

4. These are very young cows. _____

5. These people live next door to you. _____

6. These women have husbands. _____

7. These reach out from tree trunks. _____

8. You sit on these in a park. _____

9. These happen when cars hit other cars. _____

10. Collecting stamps is an example of these. _____

11. Doing these can make you stronger. _____

12. Runners and gymnasts are these. _____

13. These can be about real or made-up events. _____

14. Referees give these to rule-breakers. _____

15. These places make things to sell. _____

Rhymes

Write the spelling word that completes each sentence and rhymes
with the underlined word.

16. The workers put their <u>wrenches</u> on the _____.

17. When it was twenty _____, my nose began to <u>freeze</u>!

18. Ms. Lowe <u>teaches</u> us how to give _____.

19. Everyone loves to go to <u>Artie's</u> birthday _____.

Plural Words

stories	wives	benches	skis
calves	sandwiches	branches	athletes
parties	companies	neighbors	hobbies
exercises	penalties	degrees	vegetables
speeches	crashes	wishes	businesses

Proofreading

Proofread the paragraph below. Use proofreading marks to correct five spelling mistakes, three capitalization mistakes, and two punctuation mistakes.

Proofreading Marks

◯ spell correctly

≡ capitalize

⊙ add period

Up and Away

I learned about model airplanes from my neighbors, Victor and melinda Last Saturday we sat on the benchs in their yard, ate sandwitches, and talked about planes. They showed me their models and told storyes about each one Victor's favorite model is one that his great-grandfather gave him. It's a Spitfire, an airplane used by the Royal Air Force in World War II. Victor's great-grandfather flew a Spitfire in that war. i decided to build my own models. Victor said that of all the hobies, building model airplanes is his favorite. now it's mine, too. My father is helping me build a Spitfire and a Hornet.

Subject-Verb Agreement

The subject and the verb of a sentence must "agree" in number. A plural subject must have a plural verb. A singular subject must have a singular verb.

> **Singular Subject**   **Plural Subject**
> This **story** is about a zookeeper.   **All** of the stories are interesting.

The subject of each of the following sentences appears in dark type.
Choose the correct verb for the subject. Then write the sentence correctly.

1. My **neighbor** (was, were) upset about losing her parrot.

_____

2. The **vegetables** in our garden (is, are) ready to be picked.

_____

3. The mayor's **speech** (seem, seems) too long and too serious.

_____

4. These cucumber **sandwiches** really (does, do) taste good.

_____

5. Our **calves** (spends, spend) most of the day playing.

_____

6. The **benches** at the city park (need, needs) to be replaced.

_____

7. His father's **company** (build, builds) parts for computers.

_____

unit 2 Review
Lessons 6–10

Lesson 6

delivery
empty
athlete
evening
believe

Words with /ē/

Write the spelling word that completes each sentence.

1. The _____ trained every day.
2. Every _____ after dinner, we play a word game.
3. Tell the truth so that people will always _____ you.
4. Joe's Pizza Place has free _____ service.
5. I spent all my money, so my wallet is _____.

Lesson 7

weak
reason
breathe
speech
piano

More Words with /ē/

Write the spelling word for each clue.

6. This is a musical instrument with keys. _____
7. If something is not strong, then it's this. _____
8. Humans do this to get air. _____
9. This tells why something is the way it is.

   _____

10. You give one of these when you give a talk.

    _____

Lesson 8

different
chimney
except
enough
guilty

Words with /ĭ/

Write the spelling word for each definition.

11. a tall structure through which smoke can flow _____
12. feeling that one has done something wrong _____

13. outside of or apart from _____

14. not the same as _____

15. as much as is needed _____

kitchen
mystery
garbage
message
business

More Words with / ĭ /

Write the spelling word that completes each analogy.

16. *Trash* is to _____ as *bag* is to *sack*.

17. *Store* is to _____ as *cottage* is to *house*.

18. *Passage* is to *hall* as *letter* is to _____.

19. *Piece* is to *puzzle* as *clue* is to _____.

20. *Bedroom* is to *sleep* as _____ is to *cook*.

skis
businesses
companies
calves
wives

Plural Words

Write the spelling word that answers each question.

21. What are baby cows called? _____

22. What is another word for *businesses*? _____

23. What do people use to go down a snowy mountain?

_____

24. What do husbands have? _____

25. What can you see on the main streets of small towns?

_____

Words with /ī/

mild	library	science	guide
idea	quite	awhile	ninth
pirate	polite	tried	decide
remind	revise	island	grind
knife	climb	invite	blind

island

Say and Listen

Say each spelling word. Listen for the /ī/ sound you hear in *mild*.

Think and Sort

Look at the letters in each word. Think about how /ī/ is spelled. Spell each word aloud.

How many spelling patterns for /ī/ do you see?

1. Write the **seven** spelling words that have the *i*-consonant-*e* pattern, like *quite*.

2. Write the **eleven** spelling words that have the *i* pattern, like *mild*.

3. Write the **one** spelling word that has the *ie* pattern.

4. Write the **one** spelling word that has the *ui* pattern after a consonant other than *q*.

1. i-consonant-e Words

_____ _____ _____

_____ _____ _____

_____

2. i Words

_____ _____ _____

_____ _____ _____

_____ _____ _____

_____ _____

3. ie Word **4. ui Word**

_____ _____

Classifying

Write the spelling word that belongs in each group.

1. mathematics, reading, _____
2. lead, direct, _____
3. robber, thief, _____
4. chop, crush, _____
5. change, edit, _____
6. spear, dagger, _____
7. tested, attempted, _____
8. thought, opinion, _____
9. calm, gentle, _____
10. seventh, eighth, _____

Definitions

Write the spelling word for each definition.
Use a dictionary if you need to.

11. to go or move up   _____
12. to come to a conclusion   _____
13. unable to see   _____
14. completely or very   _____
15. to ask someone to go somewhere   _____
16. for a brief period of time   _____
17. a place with books and reference materials   _____
18. to make a person remember   _____
19. a piece of land completely surrounded by water   _____

mild	library	science	guide
idea	quite	awhile	ninth
pirate	polite	tried	decide
remind	revise	island	grind
knife	climb	invite	blind

Proofreading

Proofread this paragraph from a short story. Use proofreading marks to correct five spelling mistakes, two punctuation mistakes, and three unnecessary words.

Proofreading Marks

◯ spell correctly

? add question mark

✗ take out

The Decision

The sailor depended on the stars that twinkled in the black night sky to giude him along his course. Tonight, however, a thick fog had stolen in and a covered everything in a thick, wet blanket. The sailor had no iddea where he was, and he couldn't deside what to do. Should he drop it the ship's anchor and wait for awile Would the that just invite a pyrate attack The choice that he made in this moment could change the rest of his life.

Direct Quotations

Quotation marks are placed around the exact words of a speaker. The first word in a direct quotation begins with a capital letter. If the quotation falls at the end of a sentence, the end punctuation is placed inside the final quotation mark. A comma is usually used to set off the quotation from the rest of the sentence. Notice the capitalization and punctuation in the following examples.

> Lisa asked, "Will you come to the parade with us?"
>
> "I would love to go with you," said Bob.
>
> "Can you bring some chairs?" asked Lisa.

The following sentences contain errors in capitalization and punctuation. Write each sentence correctly.

1. Mr. Perry said my workload is easing up quite a bit

_____

2. why don't you decide to take a vacation asked Mrs. Perry

_____

_____

3. Mr. Perry answered i'd like to climb a high mountain

_____

_____

4. we should take a guide so that we won't get lost added Mr. Perry

_____

_____

Words with /ŏ/

dollar	honor	collar	closet
common	lobster	quantity	hospital
solid	copper	wander	problem
object	comma	watch	bother
bottom	shock	honest	promise

dollar

Say and Listen

Say each spelling word. Listen for the /ŏ/ sound you hear in *dollar*.

Think and Sort

Look at the letters in each word. Think about how /ŏ/ is spelled. Spell each word aloud.

How many spelling patterns for /ŏ/ do you see?

1. Write the **seventeen** spelling words that have the *o* pattern, like *dollar*.

2. Write the **three** spelling words that have the *a* pattern, like *watch*.

1. o Words

_____   _____   _____

_____   _____   _____

_____   _____   _____

_____   _____   _____

_____   _____

_____

2. a Words

_____   _____   _____

Synonyms

Write the spelling word that is a synonym for each word below.

1. clinic   _____
2. annoy   _____
3. difficulty   _____
4. usual   _____
5. firm   _____
6. lowest   _____
7. thing   _____
8. respect   _____
9. amount   _____
10. vow   _____
11. roam   _____

Clues

Write the spelling word for each clue.

12. This word describes a truthful person.   _____
13. This is a metal that turns green as it ages.   _____
14. This is a very sudden surprise.   _____
15. This is one hundred cents.   _____
16. This is a shellfish with two large front claws. _____
17. This part of a shirt goes around the neck.   _____
18. This is where clothes are kept.   _____
19. This is worn on the wrist.   _____

dollar	honor	collar	closet
common	lobster	quantity	hospital
solid	copper	wander	problem
object	comma	watch	bother
bottom	shock	honest	promise

Proofreading

Proofread the e-mail below. Use proofreading marks to correct five spelling mistakes, three capitalization mistakes, and two unnecessary words.

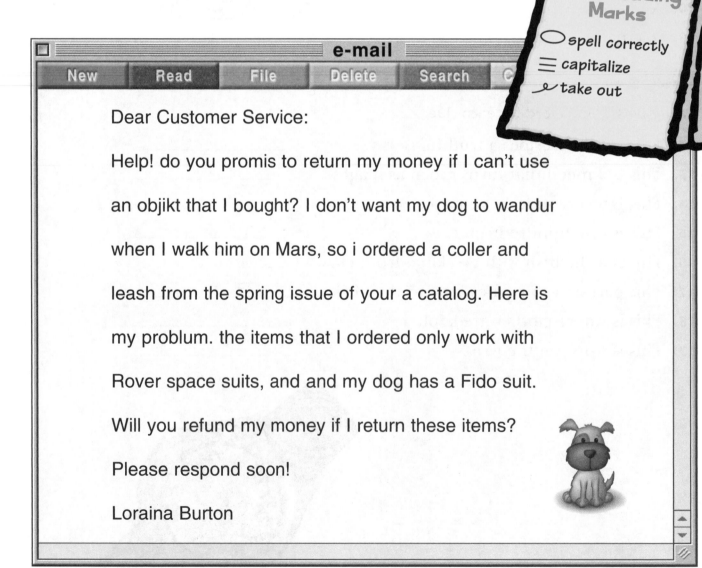

Proofreading Marks

◯ spell correctly
≡ capitalize
◞ take out

e-mail

New | Read | File | Delete | Search | C

Dear Customer Service:

Help! do you promis to return my money if I can't use

an objikt that I bought? I don't want my dog to wandur

when I walk him on Mars, so i ordered a coller and

leash from the spring issue of your a catalog. Here is

my problum. the items that I ordered only work with

Rover space suits, and and my dog has a Fido suit.

Will you refund my money if I return these items?

Please respond soon!

Loraina Burton

Simple Subjects

The simple subject of a sentence tells who or what is doing the action of the verb or is being talked about. The simple subject is the main word of the complete subject. In the following sentence, the complete subject is underlined. The simple subject appears in dark type.

> The **boy** in the blue shirt won the race.

Write the simple subject of each sentence below.

1. The local hospital was a busy place on Saturday. _____
2. Fresh lobster is a tasty meat. _____
3. A comma is a punctuation mark. _____
4. The closet in your room is a mess. _____
5. A dollar is worth ten dimes. _____
6. My new gold watch is broken. _____
7. A promise should not be broken. _____
8. The bottom of the page is empty. _____
9. The soldier's honor was at stake. _____
10. Copper is a reddish-brown metal. _____
11. The object of the game is simple. _____
12. Dina saw the deer through the trees. _____
13. The dog's collar was lying in the mud. _____
14. The engine problem can easily be solved. _____

Words with /ō/

vote	zone	known	follow
alone	microscope	arrow	grown
borrow	swallow	tomorrow	telephone
code	suppose	chose	sew
throw	bowl	owe	elbow

Say and Listen

Say each spelling word. Listen for the /ō/ sound you hear in *vote*.

Think and Sort

Look at the letters in each word. Think about how /ō/ is spelled. Spell each word aloud.

telephone

How many spelling patterns for /ō/ do you see?

1. Write the **nine** spelling words that have the *o*-consonant-*e* pattern, like *vote*.

2. Write the **ten** spelling words that have the *ow* pattern, like *arrow*.

3. Write the **one** word that has the *ew* pattern.

1. o-consonant-e Words

_____   _____   _____

_____   _____   _____

_____   _____   _____

2. ow Words

_____   _____   _____

_____   _____   _____

_____   _____

3. ew Word

_____

Classifying

Write the spelling word that belongs in each group.

1. pitch, hurl, _____
2. plate, cup, _____
3. yesterday, today, _____
4. grow, grew, _____
5. mend, stitch, _____
6. imagine, expect, _____
7. know, knew, _____
8. area, district, _____
9. dart, spear, _____
10. telescope, kaleidoscope, _____
11. picked, selected, _____
12. puzzle, signal, _____

What's Missing?

Write the missing spelling word.

13. Leave me _____!
14. Answer the _____, please.
15. _____ the leader.
16. The pill was hard to _____.
17. You _____ me a favor.
18. May I _____ your pencil?
19. Let's _____ on it.

vote	zone	known	follow
alone	microscope	arrow	grown
borrow	swallow	tomorrow	telephone
code	suppose	chose	sew
throw	bowl	owe	elbow

Proofreading

Proofread the journal entry below. Use proofreading marks to correct five spelling mistakes, three capitalization mistakes, and two mistakes in word order.

Proofreading Marks
◯ spell correctly
≡ capitalize
∿ trade places

april 8

Tommorrow I give will my science report. It's called "The Amazing microscope." I choze the microscope as a topic because have I grone very interested in tiny living things. The only way to see them is to view them through a microscope. without this important invention, we would never have knoan why people get typhoid fever and food poisoning. I suppows that we wouldn't be able to see what a flea or a mite really looks like, either. I hope everyone likes my report. I've tried to make it fun and interesting.

Verbs

The complete predicate is the part of a sentence that tells what the subject does or is. The verb is the main word or words in the predicate. In the sentences below, *Chelsey* is the subject, and the words in dark type are the verbs.

Chelsey	**will jog** to school today.
Chelsey	**is** a very good athlete.

Write each of the following sentences, correcting the spelling errors and underlining the verbs.

1. I oew Jo Anne a dollar.

_____

2. Noah can borow my bike.

_____

3. I soe my own clothes.

_____

4. Tyler and Cody folloe directions well.

_____

5. Zoey answered the telefone.

_____

6. Rosie put the slide under the microskope.

_____

More Words with /ō/

oak	hotel	coach	notice
dough	yolk	boast	poem
groan	echo	float	control
tornado	hero	coast	though
throat	clothing	scold	roast

tornado

Say and Listen

Say each spelling word. Listen for the /ō/ sound.

Think and Sort

Look at the letters in each word. Think about how /ō/ is spelled. Spell each word aloud.

How many spelling patterns for /ō/ do you see?

1. Write the **ten** spelling words that have the *o* pattern, like *yolk*.

2. Write the **eight** spelling words that have the *oa* pattern, like *oak*.

3. Write the **two** spelling words that have the *ough* pattern, like *though*.

1. o Words

_____ _____ _____

_____ _____ _____

_____ _____ _____

_____

2. oa Words

_____ _____ _____

_____ _____ _____

_____ _____

3. ough Words

_____ _____

Classifying

Write the spelling word that belongs in each group.

1. hats, shoes, _____
2. egg white, eggshell, egg _____
3. resound, repeat, _____
4. elm, birch, _____
5. ear, nose, _____
6. since, however, _____
7. direct, operate, _____
8. lecture, yell, _____
9. crust, batter, _____
10. manager, trainer, _____
11. motel, inn, _____
12. see, observe, _____
13. drift, bob, _____

Synonyms

Complete each sentence by writing the spelling word that is a synonym for the underlined word.

14. The <u>champion</u> of the chess match was our _____.
15. This _____ is <u>verse</u> that doesn't rhyme.
16. Sail along the _____ and stop near the <u>shore</u>.
17. A stomachache can make you <u>moan</u> and _____.
18. Some people <u>brag</u> and _____ when they win a game.
19. Should I <u>bake</u> the chicken and _____ the corn?

oak	hotel	coach	notice
dough	yolk	boast	poem
groan	echo	float	control
tornado	hero	coast	though
throat	clothing	scold	roast

Proofreading

Proofread the diary entry below.
Use proofreading marks to correct five
spelling mistakes, three capitalization
mistakes, and two punctuation mistakes.

Proofreading Marks

⬭ spell correctly
⁄ make lowercase
⊙ add period

Dear Diary,

Last night a tornadoe hit our Town. I've never been so scared

in all my life. I woke up around Midnight when our house began

to grone. I looked outside and saw lawn chairs and branches

flying through the air. Dad said we had to get somewhere in the

middle of the house, so we gathered in the hall Soon we heard

nothing but the roaring wind spinning out of controle. This

morning we saw that the roof of the hotell next door was gone.

The oke tree in our yard had been pulled up by the roots.

I'm grateful that We are all unharmed

Dictionary Skills

Parts of Speech

The parts of speech include noun *(n.)*, verb *(v.)*, adverb *(adv.)*, and preposition *(prep.)*. Some words can be used as more than one part of speech. The parts of speech for those words are usually listed within one dictionary entry.

> **coast** (kōst) *n.* The edge of land along the sea. —*v.* **coast·ed, coast·ing.** To move without power or effort: *coast down a hill.*

> **con·trol** (kən trōl′) *v.* **con·trolled, con·trol·ling.** To have power over: *control a country; control a car.* —*n.* **1.** Authority or power: *the athlete's control over his body.* **2. controls.** Instruments for operating a machine.

Both *coast* and *control* can be used as a noun and a verb. Use the words to complete the sentences below. Then write *noun* or *verb* after each to tell how it is used in each sentence.

1. Joan couldn't _____ the frisky pony.

_____

2. I like to _____ down the hill on my skateboard.

_____

3. We rented a house on the _____ of Florida.

_____

4. Gymnasts have remarkable _____ over their body.

_____

5. The hotel guests' fear seemed out of _____.

_____

6. We drove along the _____ today.

_____

Media Words

graphics	animation	columnist	byline
studio	earphones	producer	commercial
recorder	video	network	camera
newspaper	director	television	editorial
headline	musician	masthead	broadcast

musician

Say and Listen

Say each spelling word. Listen for the number of syllables in each word.

Think and Sort

Look at the letters in each word. Think about the number of syllables in the word. Spell each word aloud.

1. Write the **seven** spelling words that have two syllables, like *graphics*. Draw dashes between the syllables, like *graph-ics*.

2. Write the **ten** spelling words that have three syllables, like *director*. Draw dashes between the syllables.

3. Write the **three** spelling words that have more than three syllables, like *animation*. Draw dashes between the syllables.

---

1. Words with Two Syllables

_____ _____ _____

_____ _____ _____

_____

2. Words with Three Syllables

_____ _____ _____

_____ _____ _____

_____ _____ _____

_____

3. Words with More than Three Syllables

_____ _____ _____

Compound Words

Write the spelling word that is made from the two underlined words in each sentence.

1. The <u>phones</u> were close to my right <u>ear</u>. _____

2. The horse's <u>head</u> has a white <u>line</u> on it. _____

3. We walked <u>by</u> the <u>line</u> for the movie. _____

4. Lee <u>cast</u> a glance over the <u>broad</u> meadow. _____

5. I bumped my <u>head</u> on the sailboat's <u>mast</u>. _____

6. Will this <u>net</u> <u>work</u> in the river? _____

7. The reporter read the <u>news</u> from a sheet of <u>paper</u>. _____

Clues

Write the spelling word for each clue.

8. an ad on TV _____

9. someone who plays a musical instrument _____

10. a person who writes a daily or weekly feature _____

11. a newspaper column that tells the writer's opinion _____

12. a movie put on tape for viewing on television _____

13. a device for taking pictures _____

14. a way to bring drawings to life _____

15. a person who instructs movie actors and crew _____

16. a place where TV shows and movies are filmed _____

17. the person who manages the making of a TV show _____

18. a device that saves sounds on magnetic tape _____

19. artwork in a video game _____

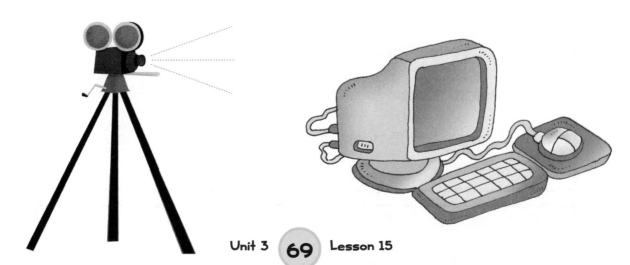

graphics	animation	columnist	byline
studio	earphones	producer	commercial
recorder	video	network	camera
newspaper	director	television	editorial
headline	musician	masthead	broadcast

Proofreading

Proofread the help-wanted ad below. Use proofreading marks to correct five spelling mistakes, three capitalization mistakes, and two mistakes in word order.

Proofreading Marks

◯ spell correctly
≡ capitalize
∼ trade places

Help Wanted!

KNBE, the most popular network in North America, is

seeking a praducer and a director for its new telavision

show. the show about is a newspaper columist and a

musician who are roommates. job requirements include a

bachelor's degree in theater arts or radio/TV, three years'

experience working on similar small-screen projects,

camara knowledge, and a stable work history. if are you

interested, contact the KNBE stewdio at 555-3054 for an

application. KNBE is an equal opportunity employer.

Capitalization

Names of cities, states, countries, bodies of water, mountains, and streets are capitalized.

> Larry visited **S**an **F**rancisco, **C**alifornia, last summer.
> He saw the **P**acific **O**cean.

The following scrambled sentences contain errors in capitalization.
Unscramble each sentence and write it correctly.

1. broadcast came The new york from.

_____

2. the was commercial rocky mountains The filmed in.

_____

3. mentioned The washington, d.c., headline virginia and.

_____

4. was arctic ocean The about newspaper the article.

_____

5. a hollywood We studio visited.

_____

6. lives director paris in The of that film.

_____

7. The show atlantic ocean television was about the.

_____

unit 3 Review
Lessons 11-15

Lesson 11

decide
island
library
ninth
science
guide

Words with /ī/

Write the spelling word that completes each analogy.

1. *Cloud* is to *sky* as _____ is to *sea*.
2. *Reside* is to *residence* as _____ is to *decision*.
3. *Eight* is to *eighth* as *nine* is to _____.
4. *Scientist* is to _____ as *historian* is to *history*.
5. *Leader* is to _____ as *path* is to *trail*.
6. *Teacher* is to *classroom* as *librarian* is to _____.

Lesson 12

collar
common
hospital
promise
wander

Words with /ŏ/

Write the spelling word that belongs in each group.

7. waistband, cuff, _____
8. doctor's office, clinic, _____
9. usual, ordinary, _____
10. guarantee, oath, _____
11. roam, drift, _____

Lesson 13

telephone
owe
borrow
sew

Words with /ō/

Write the spelling word that answers each question.

12. What can you use to call a friend? _____
13. What can you do if you forget your pencil? _____
14. How do you attach a missing button to a coat?
    _____
15. What word has the meaning "to be in debt"?
    _____

echo
notice
yolk
groan
throat
though

More Words with /ō/

Write the spelling word for each definition.

16. a repeating or bouncing sound

_____

17. a narrow passage or entryway   _____

18. even if; in spite of the fact that _____

19. a printed announcement   _____

20. to moan deeply or sadly   _____

21. the yellow part of an egg   _____

musician
camera
commercial
graphics

Media Words

Write the spelling word that completes each sentence.

22. The girl was a brilliant _____.

23. Kayla liked the _____ on her computer screen.

24. My new _____ has a zoom lens.

25. The new pizza _____ features a singing parrot.

Words with /ŭ/

crush	judge	rough	husband	tongue
pumpkin	monkey	onion	touch	hundred
jungle	compass	blood	among	knuckle
flood	instruct	country	dozen	wonderful

Say and Listen

pumpkin

Say each spelling word. Listen for the /ŭ/ sound you hear in *crush*.

Think and Sort

Look at the letters in each word. Think about how /ŭ/ is spelled. Spell each word aloud.

How many spelling patterns for /ŭ/ do you see?

1. Write the **eight** spelling words that have the *u* pattern, like *crush*.

2. Write the **seven** spelling words that have the *o* pattern, like *among*.

3. Write the **three** spelling words that have the *ou* pattern, like *touch*.

4. Write the **two** spelling words that have the *oo* pattern, like *flood*.

1. u Words

_____   _____   _____

_____   _____   _____

_____   _____

2. o Words

_____   _____   _____

_____   _____   _____

_____

3. ou Words

_____   _____   _____

4. oo Words

_____   _____

Classifying

Write the spelling word that belongs in each group.

1. courtroom, lawyer, _____

2. pepper, garlic, _____

3. desert, plains, _____

4. teeth, gums, _____

5. map, backpack, _____

6. hand, finger, _____

Clues

Write the spelling word for each clue.

7. If you pound ice into pieces, you do this.   _____

8. This red liquid is pumped through the body.   _____

9. This is a married man.   _____

10. This is a group of twelve.   _____

11. This word means "excellent."   _____

12. A wagon bounces over this kind of road.   _____

13. If you teach, you do this.   _____

14. This is ten times ten.   _____

15. This is another word for *nation*.   _____

16. When you have a lot of rain, you might get this.   _____

17. This word means "in the company of."   _____

18. This is what you don't do to a hot stove.   _____

19. This animal has hands with thumbs.   _____

crush	judge	rough	husband
tongue	pumpkin	monkey	onion
touch	hundred	jungle	compass
blood	among	knuckle	flood
instruct	country	dozen	wonderful

Proofreading

Proofread the advertisement below.
Use proofreading marks to correct five spelling
mistakes, two punctuation mistakes, and three
missing words.

Proofreading Marks

◯ spell correctly

? add question mark

∧ add

Try No-Cry!

Do you cry when peel an uniun Have you tried chilling

it, peeling it underwater, or shutting your eyes As you

know, these old-fashioned remedies don't work, but we

have a new one does. Now is the time to try No-Cry!

Just place two No-Cry pills on your tung. No tears

will stream down your face. Your eyes will not sting.

No store in the countre sells these pills, so order a

bottle now. In fact, order two. Each

bottle contains a dozan pills.

They wonderfull!

Dictionary Skills

Homographs

Some words are spelled exactly like other words but have different meanings and different origins. Some are also pronounced differently. These words are called homographs. *Homo* means "same," and *graph* means "write." Homographs appear as separate entry words in dictionaries, and they are numbered.

> **bowl¹** (bōl) *n.* **1.** A round dish used to hold things. **2.** Something shaped like a bowl.
> **bowl²** (bōl) *v.* **bowled, bowl·ing. 1.** To play the game of bowling: *Rita likes to bowl after school.* **2.** To roll a ball in the game of bowling: *Who bowls first?*

> **des·ert¹** (dĕz' ərt) *n.* A dry, sandy region.
> **de·sert²** (dĭ zûrt') *v.* **de·sert·ed, de·sert·ing.** To forsake; abandon: *She did not desert her friends when they needed her.*

Complete each sentence with one of the homographs above. Then write the entry number for the homograph.

1. May I have a _____ of soup?   _____

2. I like to _____ with my team
   on Saturdays.   _____

3. I hope I _____ a few strikes.   _____

4. The _____ had not seen rain
   in two years.   _____

5. The students walked down into the rocky
   _____ left by the meteorite.   _____

6. Don't _____ a person in need.   _____

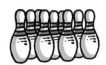

Words with /ô/

dawn	wrong	already	daughter	automobile
thought	raw	taught	bought	all right
fought	fault	autumn	often	brought
caught	straw	lawn	crawl	awful

Say and Listen

Say each spelling word. Listen for the /ô/ sound you hear in *dawn*.

Think and Sort

daughter

Look at the letters in each word. Think about how /ô/ is spelled. Spell each word aloud.

How many spelling patterns for /ô/ do you see?

1. Write the **two** spelling words that have the *a* pattern, like *already*.

2. Write the **two** spelling words that have the *o* pattern, like *wrong*.

3. Write the **three** spelling words that have the *au* pattern, like *fault*.

4. Write the **six** spelling words that have the *aw* pattern, like *dawn*.

5. Write the **seven** spelling words that have the *augh* or *ough* pattern, like *taught*.

---

1. a Words

_____   _____

2. o Words

_____   _____

3. au Words

_____   _____   _____

4. aw Words

_____   _____   _____

_____   _____   _____

5. augh, ough Words

_____   _____   _____   _____

_____   _____   _____   _____

_____

Antonyms

Antonyms are words that have opposite meanings.
Write the spelling word that is an antonym of each word below.

1. dusk _____

2. sold _____

3. right _____

4. seldom _____

5. wonderful _____

6. cooked _____

7. unsatisfactory _____

8. learned _____

Analogies

Write the spelling word that completes each analogy.

9. *Spring* is to *warm* as _____ is to *cool.*

10. *Tell* is to *told* as *catch* is to _____ .

11. *Grass* is to _____ as *leaves* are to *tree.*

12. *Fast* is to *run* as *slow* is to_____ .

13. *Fight* is to _____ as *sing* is to *sang.*

14. _____ is to *past* as *right away* is to *soon.*

15. *Eat* is to *ate* as *think* is to_____ .

16. *Mother* is to _____ as *father* is to *son.*

17. *Pillow* is to *feather* as *scarecrow* is to _____ .

18. *Asked* is to *ask* as_____ is to *bring.*

19. *Find* is to *locate* as *mistake* is to_____ .

dawn	raw	autumn	crawl
thought	fault	lawn	automobile
fought	straw	daughter	all right
caught	already	bought	brought
wrong	taught	often	awful

Proofreading

Proofread the e-mail below. Use proofreading marks to correct five spelling mistakes, three capitalization mistakes, and two punctuation mistakes.

Proofreading Marks

◯ spell correctly
≡ capitalize
⊙ add period

---

e-mail

New	Read	File	Delete	Sea

Hi, Aunt sylvia!

Did you have a good summer? I did, except for one problem. I was supposed to mow mrs. Hu's laun each week until she returned in the awtumn. She taght me how to start her mower, and I thought I had caught on. I was rong

After ten days, her yard looked auful. I finally asked a neighbor what to do. he showed me how to start the mower, and everything was fine I hope I can do it again next summer.

Raymond

Apostrophes

A contraction is a shortened form of two or more words in which one or more letters are left out. An apostrophe shows where the letters have been left out.

> had + not hadn't

A possessive noun is a noun form that shows ownership. An apostrophe and -s are used to form the possessive of a singular noun. An apostrophe and -s are also used to form the possessive of a plural noun that does not end in -s. If a plural noun ends in -s, only an apostrophe is used.

> **Singular Possessives**   **Plural Possessives**
> the dog's house   the mice's cage
>   the girls' dresses

The following sentences contain spelling errors and apostrophe errors. Write each sentence correctly.

1. Mom: Ive brawt you a surprise.

_____

2. Stuart: I thawt youd forgotten my birthday.

_____

3. Mom: Its all boys favorite means of transportation.

_____

4. Stuart: You bougt me a car like Dads!

_____

5. Mom: Youre rong, silly boy. Its a bicycle.

_____

Words with /o͞o/

choose	loose	lose	rooster
balloon	shampoo	improve	clue
kangaroo	fruit	proof	prove
truth	foolish	shoe	whom
juice	whose	raccoon	glue

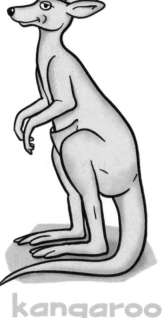

Say and Listen

Say each spelling word. Listen for the /o͞o/ sound you hear in *choose*.

Think and Sort

Look at the letters in each word. Think about how /o͞o/ is spelled. Spell each word aloud.

kangaroo

How many spelling patterns for /o͞o/ do you see?

1. Write the **nine** spelling words that have the *oo* pattern, like *choose*.

2. Write the **five** spelling words that have the *u, ue,* or *ui* pattern, like *truth*.

3. Write the **six** spelling words that have the *o*-consonant-*e, oe,* or *o* pattern, like *whom*.

1. oo Words

_____ _____ _____

_____ _____ _____

_____ _____ _____

2. u, ue, ui Words

_____ _____ _____

_____ _____

3. o-consonant-e, oe, o Words

_____ _____ _____

_____ _____ _____

Hink Pinks

Write the spelling word that completes each hink pink.

1. colored paste   blue _____

2. song sung by a masked animal   _____ tune

3. drink for large animal with antlers   moose _____

4. an unattached train car   _____ caboose

5. honesty from a ten-year-old   youth _____

6. what puppies make from footwear   _____ chew

Clues

Write the spelling word for each clue.

7. This is a form of *who*.   _____

8. An apple is this kind of food.   _____

9. You do this when you show a thing is true. _____

10. This word is a homophone for *who's*.   _____

11. People use this to wash their hair.   _____

12. A lawyer presents this to a jury.   _____

13. This is the opposite of *wise*.   _____

14. This animal crows in the morning.   _____

15. People fill this with air.   _____

16. This is the opposite of *find*.   _____

17. You do this when you pick something.   _____

18. You practice so that you will do this.   _____

19. A detective looks for this.   _____

choose	loose	lose	rooster
balloon	shampoo	improve	clue
kangaroo	fruit	proof	prove
truth	foolish	shoe	whom
juice	whose	raccoon	glue

Proofreading

Proofread the paragraph below from a book report. Use proofreading marks to correct five spelling mistakes, three capitalization mistakes, and two punctuation mistakes.

Proofreading Marks

◯ spell correctly

/ make lowercase

⊙ add period

Jeremy Garza   Benton Middle School

Fourth Period   January 5, 2003

"The Grape Mystery"

"The Grape Mystery" is a short Story by Anna Heglin

The main character is a detective named Reba Barberra.

Reba needs to solve a mystery about a Missing diamond

necklace. Reba suspects the next door neighbor, whooz wife

is going on a long voyage. Reba's clew is a spot on the floor

Someone has stepped on a grape and smashed it. Now she

has to find a shoo with Smashed fruite on the bottom of

it. Will that be enough for Reba to proove this person is

the thief?

Dictionary Skills

Pronunciation

A dictionary lists the pronunciation for each entry word. The pronunciation is written in special symbols. To know what sound each of the symbols stands for, you must refer to the pronunciation key. It lists the symbols and gives examples of words that have the sounds of the symbols.

Write the word for each pronunciation below.
Check your answers in a dictionary.

1. (ră ko͞on′)   _____

2. (jo͞os)   _____

3. (bə lo͞on′)   _____

4. (tro͞oth)   _____

5. (ĭm pro͞ov′)   _____

6. (pro͞of)   _____

7. (lo͞os)   _____

8. (ro͞o′ stər)   _____

9. (shăm po͞o′)   _____

10. (fo͞o′ lĭsh)   _____

11. (lo͞oz)   _____

12. (glo͞o)   _____

Pronunciation Key

ă	pat	ŏ	pot	ŭ	cut
ā	pay	ō	toe	ûr	urge
âr	care	ô	paw, for	ə	about,
ä	father	oi	noise		item,
ĕ	pet	o͝o	took		edible,
ē	bee	o͞o	boot		gallop,
ĭ	pit	ou	out		circus
ī	pie	th	thin	ər	butter
îr	deer	*th*	this		

HOME
SWEET
HOME

Words with /oi/

noise	destroy	annoy	enjoy
choice	appoint	moisture	employment
boiler	oyster	coin	loyal
avoid	loyalty	voice	voyage
royal	broil	employ	appointment

Say and Listen

Say each spelling word. Listen for the /oi/ sound you hear in *noise.*

Think and Sort

Look at the letters in each word. Think about how /oi/ is spelled.
Spell each word aloud.

How many spelling patterns for /oi/ do you see?

coin

1. Write the **ten** spelling words that have the *oy* pattern, like *loyal.*

2. Write the **ten** spelling words that have the *oi* pattern, like *noise.*

1. oy Words

_____ _____ _____

_____ _____ _____

_____ _____ _____

_____

2. oi Words

_____ _____ _____

_____ _____ _____

_____ _____ _____

_____

What's the Answer?

Write the spelling word that answers each question.

1. An opera singer uses what to make music? _____
2. A diver might find a pearl in what? _____
3. What do you need in order to see the doctor? _____
4. What do you want if you're looking for a job? _____
5. What do you feel when you walk barefoot on damp grass? _____
6. What is a trip on a ship called? _____
7. Where does the steam to power a steamboat come from? _____
8. You do what when you name someone to do something? _____
9. What word describes the palace of a king? _____

Synonyms

Complete each sentence by writing the spelling word that is a synonym for the underlined word.

10. Pele knew the rain would <u>wreck</u> his sand castle. _____
11. The coat with the hood is my <u>selection</u>. _____
12. Mr. Bander will <u>grill</u> hamburgers and chicken. _____
13. A dog can be a <u>faithful</u> friend. _____
14. Students who talk out of turn <u>bother</u> Mrs. Reyna. _____
15. The department store will <u>hire</u> ten new clerks. _____
16. Sam showed his <u>faithfulness</u> by keeping Ann's secret. _____
17. Jordan will do anything to <u>escape</u> yardwork. _____
18. A loud, frightening <u>sound</u> blared from the foghorn. _____
19. Ping and Sara really <u>like</u> opera music. _____

noise	destroy	annoy	enjoy
choice	appoint	moisture	employment
boiler	oyster	coin	loyal
avoid	loyalty	voice	voyage
royal	broil	employ	appointment

Proofreading

Proofread the journal entry below. Use proofreading marks to correct five spelling mistakes, two capitalization mistakes, and three unnecessary words.

Proofreading Marks

◯ spell correctly

≡ capitalize

ℓ take out

April 5

maria wants to be a doctor, and Rita hopes to be

a a ballet dancer. But I enjoye so many things that

it's hard to decide on just one career. Each day i

have a new idea and make a new choyce.

I'd like to to avoid being a singer, because my voyce

sounds more like noyze than music! I love horses, so

maybe I could work with with them. Maybe someone

would employe me to train and ride their horses.

Dictionary Skills

Syllables and Accent Marks

A syllable is a word part or a word with one vowel sound. An accent mark (′) tells which syllable in a word is spoken with more force, or stress. The pronunciations in a dictionary show the accented syllables in words.

> **loyal** (loi′əl)   **annoy** (ə noi′)

Find each word in a dictionary. Write the pronunciation of each word. Circle the accented syllable.

1. destroy _____

2. royal _____

3. moisture _____

4. appoint _____

5. oyster _____

6. avoid _____

7. loyalty _____

8. voyage _____

9. annoy _____

10. enjoy _____

11. employment _____

12. boiler _____

13. appointment _____

14. employ _____

Sports Words

cycling	track	soccer	football
professional	basketball	skin diving	skiing
Olympics	champion	volleyball	bowling
skating	golf	baseball	amateur
swimming	tennis	hockey	competition

Say and Listen

Say each spelling word. Listen for the number of syllables.

Think and Sort

soccer

Look at the syllables in each word. Think about how each syllable is spelled.
Spell each word aloud.

1. Write the **one** spelling word that is a two-word compound.

2. Write the **two** spelling words that have one syllable, like *track*.

3. Write the **ten** spelling words that have two syllables, like *cy-cling*.

4. Write the **five** spelling words that have three syllables, like *bas-ket-ball*.

5. Write the **two** spelling words that have four syllables, like *pro-fes-sion-al*.

1. Two-word Compound   **2. One-syllable Words**

_____   _____   _____

3. Two-syllable Words

_____   _____   _____

_____   _____   _____

_____   _____   _____

_____

4. Three-syllable Words

_____   _____   _____

_____   _____

5. Four-syllable Words

_____   _____

Classifying

Write the spelling word that belongs in each group.

1. blades, wheels, ice, rink, _____
2. mitt, mound, bat, bases, _____
3. snow, poles, lifts, slopes, _____
4. tee, course, hole, caddy, _____
5. puck, stick, goalie, ice, _____
6. racket, court, net, serve, _____
7. ocean, mask, fin, snorkel, _____
8. pins, strike, lanes, gutter, _____
9. race, bicycle, water bottle, helmet, _____
10. kick, goalie, ball, net, _____
11. hoop, backboard, basket, court, _____

Definitions

Write the spelling word for each definition. Use a dictionary if you need to.

12. a path or a trail _____
13. a game in which two teams hit a large ball across a net _____
14. an oval leather ball _____
15. someone who does something for pleasure, not money _____
16. someone who is paid to play a sport _____
17. moving through water by moving one's arms and legs _____
18. a person who wins first place in a contest _____
19. a contest _____

cycling	track	soccer	football
professional	basketball	skin diving	skiing
Olympics	champion	volleyball	bowling
skating	golf	baseball	amateur
swimming	tennis	hockey	competition

Proofreading

Proofread the letter below. Use proofreading marks to correct five spelling mistakes, three capitalization mistakes, and two missing words.

Proofreading Marks

○ spell correctly

≡ capitalize

∧ add

9820 Hardy trail

Englewood, CO 80155

Dear Nadia,

I am so glad we have become pen pals! There is much I want

to tell you about my family and our life in louisiana. Everyone in

my family is an athlete. Dad plays gollf and basball. Mom loves

sking. I play socer, and my sister ana the star of her trak

team. Maybe one of us will become a professional some day!

Maybe one of us will even be in the Olympics!

What does your family like do? I hope you write back soon!

Sincerely,

Sydney

Commas

Use commas in a friendly letter

- to separate the city from the state in the heading
- to separate the day from the year in the heading
- after the person's name in the greeting
- after the last word in the closing.

Casper, WY
February 4, 2003
Dear Bob,
Yours truly,

The friendly letter below contains comma errors and spelling errors. Use proofreading marks to add commas where they are needed and to correct the misspelled words.

1722 W. River Rd.

Chicago IL 60657

May 5 2004

Dear Alicia

I'm so pleased that you're coming to visit. We can certainly plan lots of time for sports. Swiming and skatting have always been my favorites. My brother is going to become a profesional baskitball player. Right now he's just an amatuer. See you soon!

Sincerely

Marta

unit 4 Review
Lessons 16-20

LESSON **16**

judge
tongue
rough
flood

Words with /ŭ/

Write the spelling word that completes each sentence and rhymes with the underlined word.

1. The mouse in the movie pretended to be _____ and <u>tough</u>.

2. Who will _____ the <u>fudge</u> at the cooking contest?

3. The _____ left behind <u>mud</u> in all the houses.

4. When Victor bit his _____, he <u>hung</u> up the phone.

LESSON **17**

all right
often
fault
awful
daughter
fought

Words with /ô/

Write the spelling word that completes each sentence.

5. It was my _____ that the dish broke.

6. The man's only child was not a son but a _____.

7. A flu virus can make you feel _____.

8. When I looked outside, everything seemed _____.

9. I like to read, so I go to the library _____.

10. Doctors have _____ long and hard to wipe out diseases.

raccoon
truth
clue
juice
whose
shoe
whom

Words with /ōō/

Write the spelling word that completes each analogy.

11. *Glove* is to *hand* as _____ is to *foot*.

12. *Mammal* is to _____ as *reptile* is to *snake*.

13. *Dark* is to *light* as *lie* is to _____.

14. *It's* is to *its* as *who's* is to _____.

15. *Flour* is to *wheat* as _____ is to *orange*.

16. *Scarlet* is to *red* as *hint* is to _____.

17. *Pencil* is to *what* as *person* is to _____.

annoy
destroy
appointment
avoid
choice

Words with /oi/

Write the spelling word for each definition. Use a dictionary if you need to.

18. something that is chosen _____

19. to bother _____

20. to make useless _____

21. to stay away from _____

22. an arrangement to meet at a specific time and place _____

cycling
amateur
champion

Sports Words

Write the spelling word that answers each question.

23. What do you call someone who plays a sport for fun?

_____

24. What sport involves riding a bike? _____

25. What do you call someone who wins first prize in a contest? _____

More Words with /ô/

score	quarrel	court	adore	roar
shore	before	reward	course	board
wore	warn	tore	export	toward
perform	fortunate	orchard	import	important

Say and Listen

Say each spelling word. Listen for the /ô/ sound you hear in *score*.

Think and Sort

orchard

Look at the letters in each word. Think about how /ô/ is spelled. Spell each word aloud.

How many spelling patterns for /ô/ do you see?

1. Write the **six** spelling words that have the *o-consonant-e* pattern, like *score*.

2. Write the **six** spelling words that have the *o* pattern, like *perform*.

3. Write the **four** spelling words that have the *a* pattern, like *warn*.

4. Write the **two** spelling words that have the *ou* pattern, like *court*.

5. Write the **two** spelling words that have the *oa* pattern, like *roar*.

1. o-consonant-e Words

_____   _____   _____

_____   _____   _____

2. o Words

_____   _____   _____

_____   _____   _____

3. a Words

_____   _____   _____

_____

4. ou Words

_____   _____

5. oa Words

_____   _____

Synonyms

Write the spelling word that is a synonym for each word below.

1. act   _____

2. love   _____

3. plank   _____

4. caution   _____

5. direction   _____

6. ripped   _____

7. argue   _____

8. earlier   _____

9. to   _____

Clues

Write the spelling word for each clue.

10. the past tense of *wear*   _____

11. where people play tennis   _____

12. what is often offered for finding a lost pet   _____

13. the number of points in a game   _____

14. where sand castles are found   _____

15. what a lucky person is   _____

16. the place to find apples   _____

17. worth noticing   _____

18. what lions and tigers do   _____

19. what people do in selling goods to another country   _____

score	quarrel	court	adore
roar	shore	before	reward
course	board	wore	warn
tore	export	toward	perform
fortunate	orchard	import	important

Proofreading

Proofread the part of a newspaper article below. Use proofreading marks to correct five spelling mistakes, three capitalization mistakes, and two punctuation mistakes.

Proofreading Marks

◯ spell correctly
≡ capitalize
⊙ add period

A Heady Discovery

In a press conference on thursday, Dr. G.Y. Nott announced an importent discovery Standing befour reporters in a derby hat with a large feather, he read the findings of a four-year study. according to Dr. Nott, the people in his study who woar funny hats usually didn't kwarrel with one another Dr. Nott added that these findings made him feel very fortunat. he himself adores funny hats.

Dictionary Skills

Multiple Pronunciations

Some words may be pronounced in more than one way. A dictionary gives all the acceptable pronunciations for these words, but the one listed first is usually the most common or the preferred.

Look at the pronunciations for *quarrel* given in the entry below. Notice that only the syllable that is pronounced in a different way is given in the second pronunciation. Say *quarrel* to yourself and see which pronunciation you use.

> **quar·rel** (**kwôr′** əl) *or* (**kwŏr′**-) *n.* A fight with words; an argument. —*v.* **quar·reled, quar·rel·ing.** To have a fight with words.

Each of the following words has more than one pronunciation. Look up each word in a dictionary. Write the complete pronunciation that you use.

1. course _____
2. score _____
3. export _____
4. import _____
5. toward _____
6. aunt _____
7. aurora _____
8. chorus _____
9. closet _____
10. compass _____
11. perfume _____
12. program _____
13. absurd _____
14. meteor _____
15. pumpkin _____
16. story _____

Words with /ûr/

skirt	purpose	earn	certain
dirty	service	furnish	early
thirteen	perfect	permit	firm
hurt	furniture	learning	heard
perfume	third	pearl	personal

dirty

Say and Listen

Say each spelling word. Listen for the /ûr/ sound you hear in *skirt*.

Think and Sort

Look at the letters in each word. Think about how /ûr/ is spelled. Spell each word aloud.

How many spelling patterns for /ûr/ do you see?

1. Write the **six** spelling words that have the *er* pattern, like *permit*.
2. Write the **five** spelling words that have the *ir* pattern, like *skirt*.
3. Write the **four** spelling words that have the *ur* pattern, like *hurt*.
4. Write the **five** spelling words that have the *ear* pattern, like *pearl*.

1. er Words

_____ _____ _____

_____ _____ _____

2. ir Words

_____ _____ _____

_____ _____ _____

3. ur Words

_____ _____ _____

_____

4. ear Words

_____ _____ _____

_____ _____

Classifying

Write the spelling word that belongs in each group.

1. fragrance, scent, _____

2. sure, positive, _____

3. spotless, flawless, _____

4. eleven, twelve, _____

5. private, inner, _____

6. late, on time, _____

7. researching, studying, _____

8. curtains, rugs, _____

9. supply, provide, _____

10. allow, let, _____

11. assistance, help, _____

12. aim, goal, _____

13. solid, hard, _____

Rhymes

Write the spelling word that completes each sentence
and rhymes with the underlined word.

14. There are <u>thirty</u> _____ shirts in the laundry.

15. I need to <u>learn</u> some ways to _____ money.

16. We _____ a <u>bird</u> singing in a tree.

17. Carmen wore a yellow <u>shirt</u> that matched her _____.

18. The <u>girl</u> found a huge white _____ in the oyster.

19. Mr. <u>Byrd</u> lives in the _____ house on the left.

skirt	purpose	earn	certain
dirty	service	furnish	early
thirteen	perfect	permit	firm
hurt	furniture	learning	heard
perfume	third	pearl	personal

Proofreading

Proofread the letter below. Use proofreading marks to correct five spelling mistakes, two punctuation mistakes, and three unnecessary words.

Proofreading Marks

◯ spell correctly
⊙ add period
✗ take out

295 Hill Drive

Billings, MT 59102

September 9, 2004

Dear Aunt Libby,

    Mom told me that when you were thurteen, you did extra chores for money She said your perpose was to to buy Grandma Dora a sertain kind of pirfume. The day you you bought it, Uncle Benny spilled the whole bottle on Grandma's skurt What a smell it must have made!

    I'm trying to earn money to buy a gift for Mom. Do you you have any ideas for me?

        Love,

        Madison

Language Connection

Adjectives

An adjective describes a noun or pronoun by telling which one, what kind, or how many.

> A **colorful** bird was singing in the **old** tree.
>
> A **big fat** cat scared it away.

The following sentences contain adjectives and misspelled words. Write the sentences, spelling the misspelled words correctly and underlining the adjectives.

1. We made new ferniture for the treehouse.

_____

2. I herd there is a fantastic movie downtown.

_____

3. The urly bird catches the worm.

_____

4. I'd like to fernish my room with large green plants.

_____

5. I hert my foot when I dropped the heavy suitcase.

_____

6. Jennifer wants a perl necklace for her birthday.

_____

Words with /âr/ or /är/

share	charge	discharge	aware
harvest	prepare	fare	alarm
farther	stare	carefully	starve
margin	depart	declare	compare
square	marbles	apartment	bare

marbles

Say and Listen

Say each spelling word. Listen for the /âr/ sounds you hear in *share* and the /är/ sounds you hear in *charge*.

Think and Sort

Look at the letters in each word. Think about how /âr/ or /är/ is spelled. Spell each word aloud.

How many spelling patterns for /âr/ and /är/ do you see?

1. Write the **ten** spelling words that have /âr/, like *share*. Circle the letters that spell /âr/.

2. Write the **ten** spelling words that have /är/, like *charge*. Circle the letters that spell /är/.

1. /âr/ Words

_____   _____   _____

_____   _____   _____

_____   _____

_____

2. /är/ Words

_____   _____   _____

_____   _____   _____

_____   _____   _____

_____

Making Connections

Complete each sentence with the spelling word that goes with the underlined group of people.

1. <u>Firefighters</u> respond to a fire _____.

2. <u>Children</u> often play the game of _____.

3. <u>Doctors</u> _____ well hospital patients.

4. <u>Bus drivers</u> collect a _____ from each passenger.

5. <u>Math teachers</u> teach about the triangle and the _____.

Clues

Write the spelling word for each clue.

6. This word describes feet without shoes or socks.   _____

7. People do this with their eyes.   _____

8. Without food, people and animals do this.   _____

9. It's good to do this for a test.   _____

10. This is how you should handle sharp things.   _____

11. People do this to see how things are alike.   _____

12. This is the outer edge of paper.   _____

13. People do this when they take part of something.   _____

14. This word is the opposite of *nearer.*   _____

15. If you know there is danger ahead, you are this.   _____

16. This is a type of home.   _____

17. A bull does this when it sees a waving cape.   _____

18. Trains do this when they leave the station.   _____

19. If you announce, you do this.   _____

share	charge	discharge	aware
harvest	prepare	fare	alarm
farther	stare	carefully	starve
margin	depart	declare	compare
square	marbles	apartment	bare

Proofreading

Proofread this paragraph from a travel article. Use proofreading marks to correct five spelling mistakes, three capitalization mistakes, and two unnecessary words.

Proofreading Marks

◯ spell correctly

≡ capitalize

ℓ take out

Sonoran Scenes

a trip through the Sonoran Desert in arizona is an

amazing experience. You don't have to travel far into this

national treasure to become awair of its beauty. Nothing

can compair to to the rich colors and gorgeous sunsets.

The the flat landscape spreads farthur than the eye can see.

although the land appears baer, it does have a variety of

plant and animal life. But it is hot. You must prepaar for

the dry and scorching heat. Tour guides constantly remind

visitors to bring lots of water.

Dictionary Skills

Multiple Meanings

Some words can be used as different parts of speech and may have more than one meaning. The dictionary entries for these words list the parts of speech and different definitions.

Study the dictionary entry below.

a·larm (ə lärm') *n.* **1.** Sudden fear caused by a feeling of danger: *The animals ran away in alarm.* **2.** A warning that danger is near. **3.** A warning signal, such as a bell: *The alarm woke me up too early.* —*v.* **a·larmed, a·larm·ing.** To frighten.

Use a dictionary to identify the part of speech for the underlined word in each sentence. Then write the number of the definition.

1. The fire <u>alarm</u> rang out in the night. _____ _____

2. The club asked Maria to be in <u>charge</u> of fundraising. _____ _____

3. The town <u>square</u> is filled with beautiful green trees. _____ _____

4. Please <u>share</u> the cookies with all the children. _____ _____

5. The farmers had an early <u>harvest</u> last year. _____ _____

6. The train will <u>depart</u> at noon. _____ _____

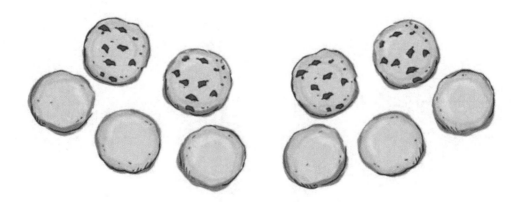

Compound Words

thunderstorm	strawberry	birthday	sailboat
cheeseburger	hallway	nightmare	notebook
upset	cartwheel	flashlight	chalkboard
grasshopper	suitcase	sawdust	uproar
weekend	homework	blueberry	breakfast

Say and Listen

Remember that a syllable is a word part or a word with one vowel sound. Say each spelling word. Listen for the number of syllables.

sailboat

Think and Sort

Each of the spelling words is a **compound word**. Because a compound word is made from two words, it has at least two syllables.

Look at the syllables in each word. Think about how each syllable is spelled. Spell each word aloud.

1. Write the **fifteen** spelling words that have two syllables, like *up-set*.

2. Write the **five** spelling words that have three syllables, like *grass-hop-per*.

---

1. Two-syllable Words

_____   _____   _____

_____   _____   _____

_____   _____   _____

_____   _____   _____

_____   _____   _____

2. Three-syllable Words

_____   _____   _____

_____   _____

Definitions

Write the spelling word for each definition.

1. the first meal of the day _____
2. a surface to write on with chalk _____
3. a hamburger with cheese _____
4. loud noise _____
5. bits of wood left over after sawing _____
6. a passageway, a walkway, or a corridor _____
7. a small red fruit with many seeds _____
8. a storm that includes lightning and thunder _____
9. a boat powered by wind _____
10. to cause someone to be worried or disturbed _____
11. schoolwork done at home or away from school _____
12. a very small blue fruit that grows on bushes _____

Compound Words

Write the spelling word that is made from the two underlined words in each sentence.

13. Sam's <u>book</u> has a <u>note</u> in it. _____
14. Dad's black <u>case</u> holds a <u>suit</u> and six pairs of jeans. _____
15. The insect in the <u>grass</u> was a <u>hopper</u>, not a crawler. _____
16. What is the <u>day</u> of your <u>birth</u>? _____
17. At the <u>end</u> of next <u>week</u>, we are going on a camping trip. _____
18. The <u>mare</u> whinnied loudly all <u>night</u>. _____
19. The clown hopped over the <u>wheel</u> of the popcorn <u>cart</u>. _____

thunderstorm	strawberry	birthday	sailboat
cheeseburger	hallway	nightmare	notebook
upset	cartwheel	flashlight	chalkboard
grasshopper	suitcase	sawdust	uproar
weekend	homework	blueberry	breakfast

Proofreading

Proofread this excerpt from a restaurant review. Use proofreading marks to correct five spelling mistakes, three capitalization mistakes, and two punctuation mistakes.

Proofreading Marks

⬭ spell correctly

≡ capitalize

⊙ add period

Restaurant Review

The Dew drop Inn is a wonderful place to eat Several friends suggested that I eat there and try the bluberry pancakes. Last wekend was my birthday, so my mother and I ate brekkfast there. The pancakes were melt-in-your-mouth moist, and the strawbury jam was delicious. just as I was jotting my thoughts in my noetbook, the waiters came out and sang "Happy birthday" to me This restaurant is a good place to go for both food and fun!

Possessive Nouns

A possessive noun is a noun that shows possession, or ownership. To form the possessive of a singular noun, add -'s. To form the possessive of a plural noun that ends in s, add only an apostrophe. If a plural noun does not end in s, add -'s to form the possessive.

Singular Possessive Nouns	Plural Possessive Nouns
Sam's notebook	the boys' homework
the mouse's fur	the women's sailboat

The sentences below contain apostrophe errors and spelling errors. Write each sentence correctly.

1. Lings flashlite was lying by the door.

_____

2. The mens' chessburgers came quickly.

_____

3. The childrens pet grasshoper was in a cage.

_____

4. Mrs. Sperrys' chalkbored was clean.

_____

5. The six performers cartwheals were magnificent.

_____

Space Words

shuttle	celestial	astronomy	revolution
comet	galaxy	axis	orbit
meteors	motion	universe	light-year
solar	rotation	telescope	asteroids
eclipse	satellite	constellation	lunar

Say and Listen

Say each spelling word. Listen for the number of syllables.

comet

Think and Sort

Look at the syllables in each word. Think about how each syllable is spelled.
Spell each word aloud.

How many syllables does each word have?

1. Write the **nine** spelling words that have two syllables, like *so-lar.*

2. Write the **eight** spelling words that have three syllables, like *u-ni-verse.*

3. Write the **three** spelling words that have four syllables, like *as-tron-o-my.*

1. Two-syllable Words

_____   _____   _____

_____   _____   _____

_____   _____   _____

2. Three-syllable Words

_____   _____   _____

_____   _____   _____

_____   _____

3. Four-syllable Words

_____   _____   _____

Classifying

Write the spelling word that belongs in each group.

1. meteor, asteroid, _____
2. mathematics, geology, _____
3. rotation, single turn, _____
4. rocket, spaceship, _____
5. microscope, gyroscope, _____

Clues

Write the spelling word for each clue.

6. the turning of Earth _____
7. a measure of distance in space _____
8. a straight line around which Earth turns _____
9. having to do with the sun _____
10. having to do with the moon _____
11. a kind of star formation _____
12. the path a planet travels around the sun _____
13. a man-made object that orbits Earth _____
14. shooting stars _____
15. relating to the heavens or skies _____
16. the Milky Way _____
17. Earth, space, and all things in it _____
18. occurs when light from the sun is cut off _____
19. a synonym for *movement* _____

Space Words

shuttle	celestial	astronomy	revolution
comet	galaxy	axis	orbit
meteors	motion	universe	light-year
solar	rotation	telescope	asteroids
eclipse	satellite	constellation	lunar

Proofreading

Proofread this paragraph from an essay. Use proofreading marks to correct five spelling mistakes, three capitalization mistakes, and two punctuation mistakes.

Proofreading Marks

◯ spell correctly
≡ capitalize
? add question mark

Space travel Far from Earth

Did you ever wonder if we could really reach other

solur systems Other stars are at least a liteyear away.

a space shuttel traveling to another star would face

many problems. it could crash into astoroids. It might

not be able to carry enough fuel for the trip. But

perhaps it could reach another galixy. What kinds of

great discoveries might we make Perhaps we would find

new planets with different types of animals and plants.

Greek and Latin Word Parts

Many English words come from Greek and Latin word parts. For example, *telescope* comes from the Greek word *tele.* Complete the chart below by writing the missing words.

Word Part	Meaning	Word	Meaning
tele	distant; far away	telescope	an instrument for viewing faraway things
uni	one	_____	everything in existence; Earth, the heavens, and all of space
		_____	an imaginary animal that looks like a white horse with a single horn on its forehead
		_____	a vehicle with one wheel
		_____	a special set of clothes that identifies the wearer as a member of one group
		_____	to make one; combine
ast	star	_____	the many small rocky bodies revolving around the sun, mainly between Mars and Jupiter
		_____	the science that deals with the sun, moon, stars, planets, and other heavenly bodies
		_____	a person who travels in a spacecraft to outer space
		_____	a star-shaped garden flower

unit 5 Review
Lessons 21-25

LESSON **21** **More Words with /ô/**

perform
fortunate
orchard
quarrel
course
board

Write the spelling word that matches each definition.
1. a flat piece of lumber _____
2. lucky _____
3. a path or direction _____
4. to do something _____
5. to argue _____
6. an area where fruit trees grow _____

LESSON **22** **Words with /ûr/**

certain
service
perfect
firm
furniture
pearl

Write the spelling word for each clue.
7. People can sleep or sit on this. _____
8. People are this when they are really sure.

   _____
9. This describes something that is hard or solid.

   _____
10. This can be found inside some oysters.

    _____
11. This is the kind of score students like to get on a test.

    _____
12. When someone does something useful, he or she

    provides this. _____

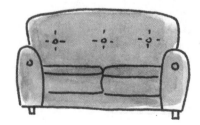

prepare
carefully
declare
compare
marbles
apartment
starve
margin

Words with /âr/ and /är/

Write the spelling word that completes each analogy.

13. *Rehearse* is to *play* as _____ is to *dinner*.

14. *Quickly* is to *slowly* as *carelessly* is to

_____.

15. *Ask* is to *question* as _____ is to *statement*.

16. *Shoot* is to _____ as *throw* is to *darts*.

17. *Stuff* is to _____ as *swell* is to *shrink*.

18. *Middle* is to *center* as *edge* is to _____.

19. *Stall* is to *horse* as _____ is to *person*.

20. *Different* is to *similar* as *contrast* is to

_____.

suitcase
nightmare

Compound Words

Write the spelling word that completes each sentence.

21. Beth's _____ was the worst
dream she'd ever had.

22. Jason forgot his black _____ at
the airport.

celestial
meteors
astronomy

Space Words

Write the spelling word that answers each question.

23. What might you see falling toward
Earth from outer space? _____

24. The moon and the stars are
what kind of bodies? _____

25. What is the science of the sun,
moon, and planets? _____

Words with /ə/

season	beautiful	perhaps	dangerous	again
citrus	ocean	canoe	banana	against
approve	chorus	qualify	mosquito	surprise
industry	cousin	government	memory	comfort

Say and Listen

Say the spelling words. Listen for the unstressed syllables with the weak vowel sound you hear at the end of *season*.

citrus

Think and Sort

The weak vowel sound in unstressed syllables is shown as /ə/. It is called **schwa**. Some words have one /ə/; others have more than one.

Look at the letters in each word. Think about how /ə/ is spelled. Spell each word aloud.

1. **Four** spelling words have two /ə/ sounds, like *banana*. Write these words and circle the letter or letters that spell each /ə/ sound.

2. Write the **five** words with /ə/ spelled *a*, like *again*.

3. Write the **one** word with /ə/ spelled *e*.

4. Write the **two** words with /ə/ spelled *i*, like *cousin*.

5. Write the **four** words with /ə/ spelled *o*, like *season*.

6. Write the **four** words with /ə/ spelled *u*, like *citrus*.

1. Two /ə/ Sounds

_____   _____   _____

_____

2. /ə/ Words with a

_____   _____

_____   _____

3. /ə/ Word with e   4. /ə/ Words with i

_____   _____   _____

5. /ə/ Words with o

_____   _____   _____

_____   _____

6. /ə/ Words with u

_____   _____   _____

_____

Synonyms

Write the spelling word that is a synonym for each word below.

1. choir _____

2. maybe _____

3. risky _____

4. shock _____

5. pretty _____

6. soothe _____

7. authorize _____

Definitions

Write the spelling word for each definition.
Use a dictionary if you need to.

8. a large body of salt water _____

9. once more _____

10. the group of people who rule a city, state, or country _____

11. a long yellow fruit _____

12. to show enough ability or skill in _____

13. the ability to remember _____

14. a small flying insect with long legs _____

15. one of the four parts of a year _____

16. a daughter or a son of an aunt or an uncle _____

17. belonging to orange or lemon trees _____

18. in an opposite direction _____

19. business, trade, and manufacturing _____

season	ocean	qualify	memory
citrus	chorus	government	again
approve	cousin	dangerous	against
industry	perhaps	banana	surprise
beautiful	canoe	mosquito	comfort

Proofreading

Proofread this paragraph from a tourist brochure. Use proofreading marks to correct five spelling mistakes, two words that are out of order, and one unnecessary word.

Proofreading Marks

◯ spell correctly
∼ trade places
ℓ take out

Maine a is beautyful state in any seasen, but fall is a truly spectacular time of year. Although the state has been given the nickname "the Pine Tree State," Maine is home to many trees whose leaves turn color every autumn. Drive along tree-lined streets and gaze in wunder at the brilliant colors the of foliage. Stand along the edge of the ocian and watch the waves crash agenst the shore. Maine will delight and surprise you. Come see why Maine is the the jewel of the Northeast.

Titles

Capitalize the first word, the last word, and all other important words in a title. Underline titles of books, movies, magazines, television programs, and newspapers. Put quotation marks around titles of short works such as book chapters, stories, poems, songs, and magazine articles.

> <u>James and the Giant Peach</u>   "How to Get Organized"

The words in parentheses after each title tell what kind of title it is. Write each title correctly.

1. a beautiful memory (book chapter)

_____

2. highlights (magazine)

_____

3. chicago tribune (newspaper)

_____

4. the canoe (book)

_____

5. computer tips for kids (magazine article)

_____

6. industry and the canadian government (book)

_____

7. stopping by woods on a snowy evening (poem)

_____

Words with /əl/

nickel	whistle	general	simple
animal	final	pickles	trouble
double	puzzle	natural	tumble
barrel	tremble	musical	example
sample	wrinkle	couple	signal

Say and Listen

Say each spelling word. Listen for the /əl/ sounds
you hear at the end of *nickel*.

 nickel

Think and Sort

Look at the letters in each word. Think about how /əl/ is spelled. Spell each word aloud.
How many spelling patterns for /əl/ do you see?

1. Write the **six** spelling words that have /əl/ spelled *al*, like *final*.

2. Write the **two** spelling words that have /əl/ spelled *el*, like *nickel*.

3. Write the **twelve** spelling words that have /əl/ spelled *le*, like *double*.

1. /əl/ Words with **al**
_____   _____   _____
_____   _____   _____

2. /əl/ Words with **el**
_____   _____

3. /əl/ Words with **le**
_____   _____   _____
_____   _____   _____
_____   _____   _____
_____   _____   _____

Clues

Write the spelling word for each clue.

1. small cucumbers   _____
2. something to copy or imitate   _____
3. a sign   _____
4. twice as much of something   _____
5. a game or a riddle to solve   _____
6. to try a small piece   _____
7. a sound made by blowing air out _____
8. a movie with songs   _____
9. not specific   _____
10. not fake   _____
11. a five-cent coin   _____

Synonyms

Write the spelling word that is a synonym for the underlined word.

12. We watched the book <u>fall</u> down the stairs.   _____
13. One <u>creature</u> at the zoo was very strange.   _____
14. Jamal could not answer the <u>last</u> question.   _____
15. The pioneer collected rainwater in a large <u>keg</u>.   _____
16. Jack and Jill are a well-known <u>pair</u>.   _____
17. Most people think playing checkers is <u>easy</u>.   _____
18. My dad had a lot of <u>difficulty</u> changing the flat tire. _____
19. The cold weather made the crossing guard <u>shiver</u>. _____

nickel	whistle	general	simple
animal	final	pickles	trouble
double	puzzle	natural	tumble
barrel	tremble	musical	example
sample	wrinkle	couple	signal

Proofreading

Proofread the newspaper article below. Use proofreading marks to correct five spelling mistakes, three capitalization errors, and two words that are out of order.

Proofreading Marks

◯ spell correctly
≡ capitalize
∼ trade places

Marbletown Tribune

Friday, october 13, 2004

The Marbletown police responded to a call late Thursday night from the manager the at generel store on bank Street. The manager reported that a couple things of had been stolen—a jar of pickles and a jigsaw puzzel. This was not the first time the manager had reported trubble at the store. Last week a dog collar and a wistle were taken from the pet display. Marbletown Police Chief marvin Cates stated that this was not a simpal case that could be solved quickly.

Language Connection

Adverbs

An adverb is a part of speech that tells how, when, where, or in what way. Adverbs tell more about verbs, adjectives, and other adverbs.

> Lauren skates **gracefully**.   Her brother dances **beautifully**.

Write the sentences below, underlining the adverbs.

1. We tremble excitedly.

_____

2. All of the animals wait obediently.

_____

3. A couple of people busily sell souvenirs.

_____

4. Suddenly the signal is given.

_____

5. Each animal steps quickly.

_____

6. The circus parade marches noisily.

_____

7. Two tall clowns dance happily.

_____

Words with /ər/

teacher	similar	actor	center
toaster	calendar	rather	character
humor	whether	discover	answer
another	silver	cellar	gather
member	polar	master	sugar

Say and Listen

Say each spelling word. Listen for the /ər/ sound you hear at the end of *teacher*.

discover

Think and Sort

Look at the letters in each word. Think about how /ər/ is spelled. Spell each word aloud. How many spelling patterns for /ər/ do you see?

1. Write the **thirteen** spelling words that have /ər/ spelled *er*, like *teacher*.

2. Write the **two** spelling words that have /ər/ spelled *or*, like *humor*.

3. Write the **five** spelling words that have /ər/ spelled *ar*, like *sugar*.

1. /ər/ Words with er

_____ _____ _____

_____ _____ _____

_____ _____ _____

_____ _____

_____

2. /ər/ Words with or

_____ _____

3. /ər/ Words with ar

_____ _____ _____

_____ _____

Classifying

Write the spelling word that belongs in each group.

1. salt, flour, _____
2. alike, same, _____
3. funniness, comedy, _____
4. gold, copper, _____
5. middle, core, _____
6. some other, one more, _____
7. reply, response, _____
8. plot, setting, _____

Analogies

Write the spelling word that completes each analogy.

9. *Basement* is to _____ as *car* is to *automobile.*
10. *Driver* is to *drive* as _____ is to *teach.*
11. *Violinist* is to *orchestra* as _____ is to *play.*
12. *Student* is to *learner* as *expert* is to _____.
13. *If* is to _____ as *comment* is to *remark.*
14. *Hot* is to *tropical* as *cold* is to _____.
15. *Bird* is to *flock* as _____ is to *club.*
16. *Heat* is to _____ as *chill* is to *refrigerator.*
17. *Recover* is to *recovery* as _____ is to *discovery.*
18. *Lake* is to *rake* as *lather* is to _____.
19. *Collect* is to _____ as *scatter* is to *spread.*

teacher	similar	actor	center
toaster	calendar	rather	character
humor	whether	discover	answer
another	silver	cellar	gather
member	polar	master	sugar

Proofreading

Proofread the e-mail below. Use proofreading marks to correct five spelling mistakes, three capitalization mistakes, and two punctuation mistakes.

Proofreading Marks

◯ spell correctly
≡ capitalize
⊙ add period

---

e-mail

New	Read	File	Delete	Search	Contacts	Check

hi, Jenny,

Guess what! I am taking dance lessons! For a long time, I didn't know wether I wanted to be an actor or a dancer The careers are similur because in both you perform for an audience. I finally decided I would rathur dance, even though ballet is hard to mastor. my mother found me a good ballet teacher. i take lessons three days a week at the ballet centur

Maria

Dictionary Skills

Idioms

An idiom is a phrase that cannot be understood by using the meanings of its individual words. In a dictionary, an idiom is sometimes listed at the end of the entry for the main word in the idiom. For example, the idiom in the following sentence is defined in the entry for *blood*.

You **make my blood boil** when you say things like that!

blood (blŭd) *n.* **1.** The red liquid that is pumped through the body by the heart. **2.** Family relationship: *My cousin and I are related by blood.* **Idioms. make one's blood boil.** To anger. **make one's blood run cold.** To frighten.

Each of the following sentences contains an idiom in dark type. Try to guess the meaning of each. Use a dictionary to help you.

1. I am **racking my brains** for the name of that movie.

_____

2. John won't answer me because he's feeling **under the weather**.

_____

3. I know he'll help me **right away** when he feels better.

_____

4. Mom says I need to **set an example** for my little brother.

_____

Words with /shən/

action	information	education	location
nation	inspection	vacation	pollution
invention	population	section	election
direction	collection	transportation	instruction
fraction	selection	mention	station

Say and Listen

Say each spelling word. Listen for the /shən/ sounds you hear in the second syllable of *action*.

fraction

Think and Sort

Look at the letters in each word. Think about how /shən/ is spelled. Spell each word aloud.

1. Many words end in /shən/. The /shən/ sounds are almost always spelled *tion*. Write the **eleven** spelling words that have a consonant before /shən/, like *action*.

2. Many words have a vowel sound before /shən/. Write the **nine** spelling words that have a vowel sound before /shən/, like *information*.

1. Consonant + /shən/ Words

_____ _____ _____

_____ _____ _____

_____ _____ _____

_____ _____

2. Vowel + /shən/ Words

_____ _____ _____

_____ _____ _____

_____ _____ _____

Definitions

Write the spelling word for each definition.

1. a stop on a bus or train route _____

2. rest time from school or work _____

3. the number of people living in a given place _____

4. an independent country _____

5. part of a whole _____

6. to briefly speak about _____

7. the act of choosing from a group _____

8. facts about a specific subject _____

9. a separated part _____

10. the means of moving from place to place _____

Base-Word Clues

Complete each sentence by writing the spelling word
that is formed from the base word in dark type.

11. Electricity was a great _____. **invent**

12. Going to college continues your _____. **educate**

13. Ming has stamps from Italy in his _____. **collect**

14. Some rivers and lakes have been spoiled by _____. **pollute**

15. The soldiers stood at attention during _____. **inspect**

16. The science fiction movie was packed with _____. **act**

17. Elena's tutor gave her extra _____. **instruct**

18. No one knows the _____ of the treasure. **locate**

19. In which _____ should we walk? **direct**

action	information	education	location
nation	inspection	vacation	pollution
invention	population	section	election
direction	collection	transportation	instruction
fraction	selection	mention	station

Proofreading

Proofread the announcement below. Use proofreading marks to correct five spelling mistakes, three capitalization mistakes, and two unnecessary words.

Proofreading Marks

◯ spell correctly
≡ capitalize
✐ take out

Pollution Solution Meeting Tonight

Tonight at City Hall, mayor Jim Bond will discuss polution in in our city. Interested citizens are invited to attend. the mayor will mension plans to provide better clean-environment educasion for the entire popullation. School Superintendent Cliff Clayton and several school principals will outline the details. Anyone with ideas for further acttion that will ensure a cleaner, healthier environment is welcome to to speak. the meeting will be held from 7:00 to 8:00 P.M. A panel discussion hosted by the Sierra Club will follow.

Colons

Use a colon between the hour and the minutes in expressions of time. Also use a colon after a word that introduces a series, or a list.

> The bus will leave the station at 9:30 A.M.
>
> The bus will stop in the following cities: Omaha, Wahoo, and Lincoln.

Write each time correctly.

1. 630 _____

2. 1210 _____

3. 245 _____

4. 905 _____

Write the sentences below, using colons correctly.

5. Some of the world's best inventions include the following the wheel, the gasoline engine, the telephone, and pizza.

_____

_____

6. Three candidates are running for election Mayor Hibbs, Mrs. Gold, and Mr. Santos.

_____

_____

7. Three topics will be covered on our test pollution, transportation, and population.

_____

_____

Homophones

road	waist	right	its
hole	whole	write	plain
waste	threw	plane	their
to	it's	there	through
too	rode	they're	two

plane

Say and Listen

Say each spelling word. Listen for the words that sound alike.

Think and Sort

All of the spelling words in this lesson are homophones. **Homophones** are words that sound alike but have different meanings.

Look at the letters in each word. Think about how the word is spelled. Spell each word aloud.

1. Write the **fourteen** spelling words that are homophone pairs, like *road* and *rode*.

2. Write the **six** spelling words that are homophone triplets, like *their*, *there* and *they're*.

1. Homophone Pairs

_____ _____ _____

_____ _____ _____

_____ _____ _____

_____ _____ _____

_____ _____

2. Homophone Triplets

_____ _____ _____

_____ _____ _____

Clues

Write the spelling word for each clue.

1. A doughnut has this in the middle. _____

2. This word is another word for *street*. _____

3. This word is the opposite of *caught*. _____

4. This word is the possessive form of *it*. _____

5. You do this with a pen or a pencil. _____

6. This word is the opposite of *wrong*. _____

7. You can use *also* instead of this word. _____

8. If you have a pair, you have this many. _____

9. This word is a contraction for *they are*. _____

10. This word is the possessive form of *they*. _____

11. Belts go around this part of the body. _____

12. Something that is simple is this. _____

13. This word is a contraction for *it is*. _____

14. This is a large machine that flies through the air. _____

Rhymes

Write the spelling word that completes each sentence and rhymes
with the underlined word.

15. The _____ <u>bowl</u> was filled with pretzels.

16. Our <u>crew</u> was the first to paddle _____ the tunnel.

17. He _____ away after he <u>showed</u> us his new bike.

18. Do not go _____ the <u>zoo</u> without me!

19. Tracey got her <u>hair</u> cut over _____.

road	waist	right	its
hole	whole	write	plain
waste	threw	plane	their
to	it's	there	through
too	rode	they're	two

Proofreading

Proofread the book review below. Use proofreading marks to correct five homophone mistakes, three capitalization mistakes, and two words that are out of order.

Proofreading Marks

⬭ spell correctly

☰ capitalize

∿ trade places

Wise Words of Warning

In there new book called It's Not Too late, Jarod Marks and emily Davis right that the future the of hole world depends our on stopping the waist of natural resources.

Marks and Davis list hundreds of actions people can take every day to help. for example, turning off the water while we brush our teeth can save millions of gallons of water per day. Marks and Davis say they're is still time to save our planet. Read It's Not Too Late. It can change your life and the world we live in.

Dictionary Skills

Using the Spelling Table

A spelling table can help you find the spelling of a word in a dictionary. Suppose you are not sure how the vowel sound in *prove* is spelled. You can use a spelling table to find the different spellings for the sound. First, find the pronunciation symbol for the sound. Then read the first spelling listed for /o͞o/, and look up *proo* words in a dictionary. Look for each spelling in the dictionary until you find the correct one.

Sound	Spellings	Examples
/o͞o/	oo ew u u_e ue o o_e oe ou ui	loose, grew, truth, presume, clue, whom, prove, shoe, soup, fruit

Write the correct spelling for each word. Use the Spelling Table on page 141 and a dictionary.

1. /gŏlf/ _____

2. /klo͞o/ _____

3. /dĭ **stroi′**/ _____

4. /ûrn/ _____

5. /pə **līt′**/ _____

6. /sēj/ _____

7. /pĭ **kän′**/ _____

8. /ē′ zəl/ _____

9. /fyo͞od/ _____

10. /kōd/ _____

unit 6 review
Lessons 26-30

Lesson 26

ocean
against
surprise
mosquito
beautiful
dangerous

Words with /ə/

Write the spelling word that completes each sentence.

1. We ended our day at the beach by watching a _____ sunset.
2. My birthday party was a complete _____.
3. Driving in a blizzard can be very _____.
4. A _____ buzzed in my ear all night long.
5. If you want to go deep-sea fishing, you must travel out on the _____.
6. Push firmly _____ the door to open it.

Lesson 27

general
natural
barrel
couple
example

Words with /əl/

Write the spelling word for each definition.

7. a large, round wooden container _____
8. made by nature _____
9. two of a kind; a pair _____
10. common to most people _____
11. a sample or a model _____

Lesson 28

character
whether
humor
similar
calendar

Words with /ər/

Write the spelling word for each clue.

12. This word means "like something else." _____
13. Comedians use this to entertain an audience. _____
14. This can help you keep track of the date. _____

15. This is a person in a book, movie, or play.

_____

16. _If_ is a synonym for this word. _____

invention
direction
collection
education

Words with /shən/

Write the spelling word that completes each analogy.

17. _Collect_ is to _____ as _select_ is to _selection_.

18. _College_ is to _____ as _hospital_ is to _operation_.

19. _Eight_ is to _number_ as _north_ is to _____ .

20. _Planet_ is to _discovery_ as _light bulb_ is to _____ .

its
it's
their
there
they're

Homophones

Write the spelling word that belongs in each group.

21. we're, you're, _____

22. she's, he's, _____

23. our, your, _____

24. his, hers, _____

25. where, here, _____

commonly misspelled words

again	except	other	through
a lot	exciting	outside	today
always	family	people	together
another	favorite	piece	tomorrow
beautiful	finally	please	too
because	first	pretty	tried
been	friend	probably	until
before	friends	read	upon
beginning	getting	really	usually
believe	goes	right	vacation
birthday	guess	said	very
bought	happened	scared	want
buy	heard	school	weird
children	himself	sent	were
clothes	hospital	should	we're
come	house	since	when
cousin	into	some	where
decided	it's	sometimes	which
different	know	surprise	whole
doesn't	little	their	would
eighth	many	there	write
enough	might	they	writing
especially	morning	they're	wrote
every	myself	though	your
everyone	once	threw	you're

spelling Table

Sound	Spellings	Examples	Sound	Spellings	Examples
/ă/	a ai au	rapid, plaid, aunt	/ŏ/	o a	shock, watch
/ā/	a a_e ai ay ea eigh ey	bakery, snake, brain, delay, break, weigh, surveyor	/ō/	o o_e oa oe ou ough ow ew	hero, code, boast, toe, boulder, dough, throw, sew
/ä/	a	pecan	/oi/	oi oy	coin, enjoy
/âr/	are air ere eir	aware, fair, there, their	/ô/	a au aw o ough o_e ou oa	already, autumn, raw, often, thought, score, court, roar
/b/	b bb	bench, hobby			
/ch/	ch tch t	orchard, watch, amateur			
/d/	d dd	dawn, meddle	/o͝o/	oo o ou u	rookie, wolf, could, education
/ĕ/	e ea a ai ie ue	bench, health, many, again, friend, guess	/o͞o/	oo ew u u_e ue o o_e oe ou ui	loose, grew, truth, presume, clue, whom, prove, shoe, soup, fruit
/ē/	e e_e ea ee ei eo ey i ie y	female, theme, weak, greet, deceive, people, monkey, ski, believe, tardy			
			/ou/	ou ow	ours, towel
			/p/	p pp	party, grasshopper
/f/	f ff gh ph	film, different, laugh, elephant	/r/	r rr wr	raw, tomorrow, wrong
			/s/	s ss c	solid, message, century
/g/	g gg	golf, jogging	/sh/	sh s ce ci	wishes, sugar, ocean, special
/h/	h wh	here, whole			
/ĭ/	i a e ee u ui y	riddle, damage, relax, been, business, build, mystery	/shən/	tion	competition
			/t/	t tt ed	too, bottom, thanked
			/th/	th	though
/ī/	i i_e ie igh uy y eye	climb, quite, die, right, buy, recycle, eye	/th/	th	think
			/ŭ/	u o o_e oe oo ou	crush, dozen, become, does, blood, touch
/îr/	er ear eer eir ere yr	periodical, hear, cheer, weird, here, lyrics	/ûr/	ear er ere ir or our ur	earn, certain, were, firm, world, flourish, curve
/j/	j g dg	jot, gentle, pledge			
/k/	k c ck ch	kitchen, canoe, chicken, character	/v/	v f	vote, of
			/w/	w wh o	wish, wheat, once
/ks/	x	expert	/y/	y	yolk
/kw/	qu	quick	/yo͞o/	eau eu u u_e	beautiful, feud, mutual, use
/l/	l ll	library, pollution			
/m/	m mb mm mn	male, comb, common, condemn	/z/	z zz s	zone, quizzical, busy
			/zh/	s	treasure
/n/	n kn nn	needle, knife, pinnacle	/ə/	a e i o u	against, elephant, furniture, actor, beautiful
/ng/	n ng	wrinkle, skating			

141

Page 8
1. act, sandwich, traffic, magic, chapter, rabbit, snack, rapid, plastic, calf, program, planet, crash, salad, factory, magnet, half, crack
2. laughter, aunt

Page 9
1. planet
2. factory
3. traffic
4. calf
5. laughter
6. program
7. plastic
8. act
9. rapid
10. half
11. magnet
12. snack
13. crash
14. crack
15. aunt
16. salad
17. rabbit
18. chapter
19. magic

Page 10
Spell correctly: rapid, crash, sandwich, snack, laughter
Capitalize: Andy, I, It
Add period: after "my dad"; after "plastic wrapper"

Page 11
1. half, plastic, rabbit, traffic
2. act, aunt, planet, program
3. calf, chapter, crack, factory
4. magic, magnet, salad, sandwich
5. laughter, length, library, loose
6. rabbit, raccoon, rapid, raw

Page 12
1. scale, parade, escape, snake, male, female
2. bakery
3. paid, brain, raise, explain, holiday, remain, complain, container, delay
4. weigh, weight, neighbor
5. break

Page 13
1. snake
2. weigh
3. break
4. explain
5. remain
6. parade
7. container
8. raise
9. complain
10. holiday
11. brain
12. paid
13. scale
14. weight
15. female
16. neighbor
17. bakery
18. male
19. delay

Page 14
Spell correctly: neighbor, male, container, remain, escape
Capitalize: Pete, He, Having
Add period: after "snake Toby"; after "at Pete's house"

Page 15
1. Our class planned a holiday vacation.
2. Mr. Peterson bought fresh bread at the bakery.
3. Watch out for that snake by your foot!
4. What did you do on your break from school?

Page 16
1. bench, intend, invent, sentence, self, questions, address, checkers, depth
2. healthy, thread, wealth, weather, instead, measure, breath, pleasure, sweater, treasure
3. friendly

Page 17
1. sweater
2. thread
3. address
4. treasure
5. depth
6. healthy
7. friendly
8. questions
9. checkers
10. measure
11. bench
12. wealth
13. weather
14. breath
15. self
16. intend
17. invent
18. instead
19. pleasure

Page 18
Spell correctly: checkers, weather, instead, friendly, questions
Capitalize: Because, Beth
Add: the (between "for" and "annual"); in (between "meet" and "Memphis"); a (between "home" and "trophy")

Page 19
Guide words will vary according to dictionary.
1. address
2. bench
3. intend
4. measure
5. sentence
6. wealth

Page 20
1. century, extra, selfish, petal, length, metal, metric, wreck, special
2. else, remember, pledge, exercise, elephant, energy, desert, expert, excellent, vegetable, gentle

Page 21
1. vegetable
2. desert
3. selfish
4. excellent
5. petal
6. wreck
7. century
8. length
9. remember
10. metal
11. metric
12. gentle
13. extra
14. else
15. special
16. exercise
17. energy
18. pledge
19. expert

Page 22
Spell correctly: expert, remember, exercise, energy, excellent
Add period: after "her work"; after "555-6262"
Take out: extra "is" in first sentence; extra "of" in fourth sentence; unnecessary "a" between "give" and "an"

Page 23
1. We drove through the (desert) last (week).
2. The (divers) swam down to the (wreck).
3. (Elephants) are large (animals) from (Africa).
4. (Andy) ran the (length) of the (field).
5. (Jill) ate every (vegetable) on her (plate).
6. I can't remember where I put my (pen) and (paper).
7. (Explorers) began to circle the (globe) in the seventeenth (century).

Page 24
1. March, June, May
2. Thursday, Monday, April, Wednesday, August, Tuesday, Sunday, July, Friday
3. October, November, September, December, Saturday
4. January, February
5. St.

Page 25
1. March
2. June
3. May
4. September
5. Monday
6. Tuesday
7. Sunday
8. St.
9. January
10. Friday
11. November
12. Thursday
13. October
14. April
15. Saturday
16. Wednesday
17. February
18. December
19. July

Page 26
Spell correctly: St., Monday, October, Tuesday, November
Capitalize: Dear, Mr., Han's
Add period: after "sounds great"; after "November 11"

Page 27
1. recede
2. ailment
3. easel
4. built
5. mystery
6. laughter
7. lunar
8. comet
9. cousin
10. breath
11. friendly
12. busy
13. bridge
14. relax
15. ski
16. guide

Pages 28–29
1. half
2. factory
3. sandwich
4. laughter
5. parade
6. bakery
7. neighbor
8. holiday
9. escape
10. break
11. container
12. friendly
13. breath
14. treasure
15. wealth
16. depth
17. vegetable
18. excellent
19. length
20. special
21. exercise
22. February
23. Tuesday
24. Saturday
25. January

Page 30
1. hobby, delivery, angry, tardy, fancy, merry, pretty, penalty, ugly, liberty, empty, shady, busy
2. compete, evening, trapeze, athlete, theme, complete
3. believe

Page 31
1. trapeze
2. theme
3. ugly
4. empty
5. hobby
6. believe
7. shady
8. evening
9. penalty
10. delivery
11. liberty
12. pretty
13. angry
14. tardy
15. fancy
16. merry
17. busy
18. complete
19. compete

Page 32
Spell correctly: evening, busy, empty, ugly, believe
Capitalize: Friday, To
Add: on (between "life" and "other"); a (between "surprise" and "Martian")

Page 33
1. adjective; fully equipped
2. verb; to remove the contents of
3. verb; to finish
4. adjective; containing nothing
5. adjective; whole
6. adjective; without meaning

Page 34
1. weak, breathe, increase, peace, defeat, reason, wheat, beneath
2. greet, freeze, speech, asleep, needle, steep, sheet, agree, degree
3. pizza, piano, ski

Page 35
1. needle
2. ski
3. breathe
4. increase
5. defeat
6. beneath
7. wheat
8. pizza
9. degree
10. piano
11. sheet
12. peace
13. speech
14. weak
15. steep
16. reason
17. greet
18. freeze
19. asleep

Page 36
Spell correctly: breathe, reason, wheat, pizza, sheet
Capitalize: I, That, A
Take out: to (between "his" and "bakery"); am (between "I" and "want")

Page 37
Phrases below indicate the complete predicate and should be circled.
1. is difficult to <u>defeat</u>
2. will <u>ski</u> down these snowy mountains every winter
3. listened to the principal's farewell <u>speech</u>
4. is much too <u>steep</u> to climb
5. began to <u>freeze</u> at midnight
6. <u>agree</u> on the date for Maria's surprise party
7. can <u>greet</u> him at the door

Page 38
1. wrist, chimney, riddle, bridge, since, disease, quit, quickly, different, discuss, divide
2. expect, enough, except, relax, review
3. equipment
4. guitar, guilty, built

Page 39
1. bridge
2. wrist
3. divide
4. guilty
5. chimney
6. quit
7. quickly
8. different
9. relax
10. review
11. enough
12. built
13. equipment
14. guitar
15. riddle
16. since
17. expect
18. discuss
19. except

Page 40
Spell correctly: since, different, quickly, relax, quit
Capitalize: You, I, Ted
Add period: after "the keyboard"; after "started lessons"

Page 41
1. I broke my wrist last April. or Last April I broke my wrist.
2. We've had our trampoline since February.
3. Let's discuss where we'll go on our field trip in June.
4. Dad built a new chimney on our house last September.
5. We can expect really hot weather in July and August.
6. I need to review my notes before our test on Tuesday.
7. We'll go to a different movie theater next Saturday.

Page 42
1. skill, chicken, arithmetic, film, picnic, kitchen, sixth, pitch, insect, insist, timid
2. system, mystery
3. package, message, damage, garbage, cottage
4. village
5. business

Page 43
1. chicken
2. pitch
3. film
4. arithmetic
5. kitchen
6. package
7. system
8. picnic
9. village
10. garbage
11. cottage
12. sixth
13. timid
14. message
15. damage
16. skill
17. insist
18. insect
19. business

Page 44
Spell correctly: kitchen, timid, insect, garbage, picnic
Capitalize: Our, He, I
Add period: after "the glass"; after "scared me"

Page 45
1. I need a pencil, an eraser, and some paper to do my arithmetic.
2. Chicken can be fried, broiled, or baked.
3. We saw tulips, roses, and daisies outside the cottage.
4. The village had a bakery, a post office, and a town hall.
5. Lynn wanted to study history, business, and medicine.
6. The timid elephant was afraid of mice, snakes, and his own shadow!

Page 46
1. skis, athletes, neighbors, exercises, degrees, vegetables
2. benches, sandwiches, branches, speeches, crashes, wishes, businesses
3. stories, wives, calves, parties, companies, hobbies, penalties

Page 47
1. vegetables
2. skis
3. sandwiches
4. calves
5. neighbors
6. wives
7. branches
8. benches
9. crashes
10. hobbies
11. exercises
12. athletes
13. stories
14. penalties
15. companies
16. benches
17. degrees
18. speeches
19. parties

Page 48
Spell correctly: neighbors, benches, sandwiches, stories, hobbies
Capitalize: Melinda, I, Now
Add period: after "and Melinda"; after "each one"

Page 49
1. My neighbor was upset about losing her parrot.
2. The vegetables in our garden are ready to be picked.
3. The mayor's speech seems too long and too serious.
4. These cucumber sandwiches really do taste good.
5. Our calves spend most of the day playing.
6. The benches at the city park need to be replaced.
7. His father's company builds parts for computers.

Pages 50–51
1. athlete
2. evening
3. believe
4. delivery
5. empty
6. piano
7. weak
8. breathe
9. reason
10. speech

11. chimney
12. guilty
13. except
14. different
15. enough
16. garbage
17. business
18. message
19. mystery
20. kitchen
21. calves
22. companies
23. skis
24. wives
25. businesses

Page 52
1. quite, awhile, polite, decide, revise, knife, invite
2. mild, library, science, idea, ninth, pirate, remind, island, grind, climb, blind
3. tried
4. guide

Page 53
1. science
2. guide
3. pirate
4. grind
5. revise
6. knife
7. tried
8. idea
9. mild
10. ninth
11. climb
12. decide
13. blind
14. quite
15. invite
16. awhile
17. library
18. remind
19. island

Page 54
Spell correctly: guide, idea, decide, awhile, pirate
Add question mark: after "awhile"; after "attack"
Take out: a (between "and" and "covered"); it (between "drop" and "the"); the (between "would" and "that")

Page 55
1. Mr. Perry said, "My work-load is easing up quite a bit."
2. "Why don't you decide to take a vacation?" asked Mrs. Perry.
3. Mr. Perry answered, "I'd like to climb a high mountain."
4. "We should take a guide so that we won't get lost," added Mr. Perry.

Page 56
1. dollar, honor, collar, closet, common, lobster, hospital, solid, copper, problem, object, comma, bother, bottom, shock, honest, promise
2. quantity, wander, watch

Page 57
1. hospital
2. bother
3. problem
4. common
5. solid
6. bottom
7. object
8. honor
9. quantity
10. promise
11. wander
12. honest
13. copper
14. shock
15. dollar
16. lobster
17. collar
18. closet
19. watch

Page 58
Spell correctly: promise, object, wander, collar, problem
Capitalize: Do, I, The
Take out: a (between "your" and "catalog"); and (between "and" and "my")

Page 59
1. hospital
2. lobster
3. comma
4. closet
5. dollar
6. watch
7. promise
8. bottom
9. honor
10. Copper
11. object
12. Dina
13. collar
14. problem

Page 60
1. vote, zone, alone, microscope, telephone, code, suppose, chose, owe
2. known, follow, arrow, grown, borrow, swallow, tomorrow, throw, bowl, elbow
3. sew

Page 61
1. throw
2. bowl
3. tomorrow
4. grown
5. sew
6. suppose
7. known
8. zone
9. arrow
10. microscope
11. chose
12. code
13. alone
14. telephone
15. Follow
16. swallow
17. owe
18. borrow
19. vote

Page 62
Spell correctly: Tomorrow, chose, grown, known, suppose
Capitalize: April, Microscope, Without
Trade places: give/will, have/I

Page 63
1. I owe Jo Anne a dollar.
2. Noah can borrow my bike.
3. I sew my own clothes.
4. Tyler and Cody follow directions well.
5. Zoey answered the telephone.
6. Rosie put the slide under the microscope.

Page 64
1. hotel, notice, yolk, poem, echo, control, tornado, hero, clothing, scold
2. oak, coach, boast, groan, float, coast, throat, roast
3. dough, though

Page 65
1. clothing
2. yolk
3. echo
4. oak
5. throat
6. though
7. control
8. scold
9. dough
10. coach
11. hotel
12. notice
13. float
14. hero
15. poem
16. coast
17. groan
18. boast
19. roast

Page 66
Spell correctly: tornado, groan, control, hotel, oak
Make lowercase: town, midnight, we
Add period: after "the hall"; after "all unharmed"

Page 67
1. control/verb
2. coast/verb
3. coast/noun
4. control/noun
5. control/noun
6. coast/noun

Page 68
1. graph-ics
by-line
ear-phones
net-work
head-line
mast-head
broad-cast
2. col-um-nist
stu-di-o
pro-duc-er
com-mer-cial
re-cord-er
vid-e-o
cam-er-a
news-pa-per
di-rec-tor
mu-si-cian
3. an-i-ma-tion
tel-e-vi-sion
ed-i-tor-i-al

Page 69
1. earphones
2. headline
3. byline
4. broadcast
5. masthead
6. network
7. newspaper
8. commercial
9. musician
10. columnist
11. editorial
12. video
13. camera
14. animation
15. director
16. studio
17. producer
18. recorder
19. graphics

Page 70
Spell correctly: producer, television, columnist, camera, studio
Capitalize: The, Job, If
Trade places: about/is, are/you

Page 71
1. The broadcast came from New York.
2. The commercial was filmed in the Rocky Mountains.
3. The headline mentioned Virginia and Washington, D.C.
4. The newspaper article was about the Arctic Ocean.
5. We visited a Hollywood studio.
6. The director of that film lives in Paris.
7. The television show was about the Atlantic Ocean.

Page 72–73
1. island
2. decide
3. ninth
4. science
5. guide
6. library
7. collar
8. hospital
9. common
10. promise
11. wander
12. telephone
13. borrow
14. sew
15. owe
16. echo
17. throat
18. though
19. notice
20. groan
21. yolk
22. musician
23. graphics
24. camera
25. commercial

Page 74
1. crush, judge, husband, pumpkin, hundred, jungle, knuckle, instruct
2. tongue, monkey, onion, compass, among, dozen, wonderful
3. rough, touch, country
4. blood, flood

Page 75
1. judge
2. onion
3. jungle
4. tongue
5. compass
6. knuckle
7. crush
8. blood
9. husband
10. dozen
11. wonderful
12. rough
13. instruct
14. hundred
15. country
16. flood
17. among
18. touch
19. monkey

Page 76
Spell correctly: onion, tongue, country, dozen, wonderful
Add question mark after: "peel an onion"; "your eyes"
Add: you (between "when" and "peel"); that (between "one" and "does"); are (between "They" and "wonderful")

Page 77
1. bowl, 1
2. bowl, 2
3. bowl, 2
4. desert, 1
5. bowl, 2
6. desert, 2

Page 78
1. all right, already
2. wrong, often
3. autumn, fault, automobile
4. dawn, raw, crawl, lawn, straw, awful
5. thought, fought, daughter, caught, bought, brought, taught

Page 79
1. dawn
2. bought
3. wrong
4. often
5. awful
6. raw
7. all right
8. taught
9. autumn
10. caught
11. lawn
12. crawl
13. fought
14. Already
15. thought
16. daughter
17. straw
18. brought
19. fault

Page 80
Spell correctly: lawn, autumn, taught, wrong, awful
Capitalize: Sylvia, Mrs., He
Add period: after "was wrong"; after "was fine"

Page 81
1. Mom: I've brought you a surprise.
2. Stuart: I thought you'd forgotten my birthday.
3. Mom: It's all boys' favorite means of transportation.
4. Stuart: You bought me a car like Dad's!
5. Mom: You're wrong, silly boy. It's a bicycle.

Page 82
1. choose, loose, rooster, balloon, shampoo, kangaroo, proof, foolish, raccoon
2. clue, fruit, truth, juice, glue
3. lose, improve, prove, shoe, whom, whose

Page 83
1. glue
2. raccoon
3. juice
4. loose
5. truth
6. shoe
7. whom
8. fruit
9. prove
10. whose
11. shampoo
12. proof
13. foolish
14. rooster
15. balloon
16. lose
17. choose
18. improve
19. clue

Page 84
Spell correctly: whose, clue, shoe, fruit, prove
Make lowercase: story, missing, smashed
Add period: after "Anna Heglin"; after "the floor"

Page 85
1. raccoon
2. juice
3. balloon
4. truth
5. improve
6. proof
7. loose
8. rooster
9. shampoo
10. foolish
11. lose
12. glue

Page 86
1. destroy, annoy, enjoy, employment, oyster, loyal, loyalty, voyage, royal, employ
2. noise, choice, appoint, moisture, boiler, coin, avoid, voice, broil, appointment

Page 87
1. voice
2. oyster
3. appointment
4. employment
5. moisture
6. voyage
7. boiler
8. appoint
9. royal
10. destroy
11. choice
12. broil
13. loyal
14. annoy
15. employ
16. loyalty
17. avoid
18. noise
19. enjoy

Page 88
Spell correctly: enjoy, choice, voice, noise, employ
Capitalize: Maria, I
Take out: a (between "a" and "ballet"); to (between "to" and "avoid"); with (between "with" and "them")

Page 89
1. di(stroi)
2. (roi)əl
3. (mois)chər
4. ə(point)
5. (oi)stər
6. ə(void)
7. (loi)əl tē
8. (voi) ĭj
9. ə(noi)
10. ĕn(joi)
11. ĕm(ploi)mənt
12. (boi)lər
13. ə(point)mənt
14. ĕm(ploi)

Page 90
1. skin diving
2. track, golf
3. cycling, soccer, football, skiing, bowling, skating, baseball, swimming, tennis, hockey
4. basketball, Olympics, champion, volleyball, amateur
5. professional, competition

Page 91
1. skating
2. baseball
3. skiing
4. golf
5. hockey
6. tennis
7. skin diving
8. bowling
9. cycling
10. soccer
11. basketball
12. track
13. volleyball
14. football
15. amateur
16. professional
17. swimming
18. champion
19. competition

Page 92
Spell correctly: golf, baseball, skiing, soccer, track
Capitalize: Trail, Louisiana, Ana
Add: is (between "Ana" and "the"); to (between "like" and "do")

Page 93
Add a comma after: Chicago, May 5, Alicia, Sincerely
Spell correctly: Swimming, skating, professional, basketball, amateur

Page 94–95
1. rough
2. judge
3. flood
4. tongue
5. fault
6. daughter
7. awful
8. all right
9. often
10. fought
11. shoe
12. raccoon
13. truth
14. whose
15. juice
16. clue
17. whom
18. choice
19. annoy
20. destroy

21. avoid
22. appointment
23. amateur
24. cycling
25. champion

Page 96
1. score, adore, shore, before, wore, tore
2. export, perform, fortunate, orchard, import, important
3. quarrel, reward, warn, toward
4. court, course
5. roar, board

Page 97
1. perform
2. adore
3. board
4. warn
5. course
6. tore
7. quarrel
8. before
9. toward
10. wore
11. court
12. reward
13. score
14. shore
15. fortunate
16. orchard
17. important
18. roar
19. export

Page 98
Spell correctly: important, before, wore, quarrel, fortunate
Capitalize: Thursday, According, He
Add period: after "discovery"; after "one another"

Page 99
Answers will vary.

Page 100
1. certain, service, perfect, permit, perfume, personal
2. skirt, dirty, thirteen, firm, third
3. purpose, furnish, hurt, furniture
4. earn, early, learning, heard, pearl

Page 101
1. perfume
2. certain
3. perfect
4. thirteen
5. personal
6. early
7. learning
8. furniture
9. furnish
10. permit
11. service
12. purpose
13. firm
14. dirty
15. earn
16. heard
17. skirt
18. pearl
19. third

Page 102
Spell correctly: thirteen, purpose, certain, perfume, skirt
Add period: after "for money"; after "Grandma's skirt"
Take out: to (between "to" and "buy"); you (between "you" and "bought"); you (between "you" and "have")

Page 103
1. We made new furniture for the treehouse.
2. I heard there is a fantastic movie downtown.

3. The early bird catches the worm.
4. I'd like to furnish my room with large green plants.
5. I hurt my foot when I dropped the heavy suitcase.
6. Jennifer wants a pearl necklace for her birthday.

Page 104
1. share, aware, prepare, fare, stare, carefully, declare, compare, square, bare
2. charge, discharge, harvest, alarm, farther, starve, margin, depart, marbles, apartment

Page 105
1. alarm
2. marbles
3. discharge
4. fare
5. square
6. bare
7. stare
8. starve
9. prepare
10. carefully
11. compare
12. margin
13. share
14. farther
15. aware
16. apartment
17. charge
18. depart
19. declare

Page 106
Spell correctly: aware, compare, farther, bare, prepare
Capitalize: A, Arizona, Although
Take out: to (between "to" and "the"); the (between "the" and "flat")

Page 107
1. noun
2. noun
3. noun
4. verb
5. noun
6. verb
The number of the definition will vary.

Page 108
1. birthday, sailboat, hallway, nightmare, notebook, upset, cartwheel, flashlight, chalkboard, suitcase, sawdust, uproar, weekend, homework, breakfast
2. thunderstorm, strawberry, cheeseburger, grasshopper, blueberry

Page 109
1. breakfast
2. chalkboard
3. cheeseburger
4. uproar
5. sawdust
6. hallway
7. strawberry
8. thunderstorm
9. sailboat
10. upset
11. homework
12. blueberry
13. notebook
14. suitcase
15. grasshopper
16. birthday
17. weekend
18. nightmare
19. cartwheel

Page 110
Spell correctly: blueberry, weekend, breakfast, strawberry, notebook

Capitalize: Drop, Just, Birthday
Add period: after "to eat"; after "to me"

Page 111
1. Ling's flashlight was lying by the door
2. The men's cheeseburgers came quickly.
3. The children's pet grasshopper was in a cage.
4. Mrs. Sperry's chalkboard was clean.
5. The six performers' cartwheels were magnificent.

Page 112
1. shuttle, comet, axis, orbit, motion, light-year, solar, eclipse, lunar
2. celestial, galaxy, meteors, universe, rotation, telescope, asteroids, satellite
3. astronomy, revolution, constellation

Page 113
1. comet
2. astronomy
3. revolution
4. shuttle
5. telescope
6. rotation
7. light-year
8. axis
9. solar
10. lunar
11. constellation
12. orbit
13. satellite
14. meteors
15. celestial
16. galaxy
17. universe
18. eclipse
19. motion

Page 114
Spell correctly: solar, light-year, shuttle, asteroids, galaxy
Capitalize: Travel, A, It
Add question mark: after "solar systems"; after "we make"

Page 115
1. universe
2. unicorn
3. unicycle
4. uniform
5. unify, unite
6. asteroids
7. astronomy
8. astronaut
9. aster

Page 116–117
1. board
2. fortunate
3. course
4. perform
5. quarrel
6. orchard
7. furniture
8. certain
9. firm
10. pearl
11. perfect
12. service
13. prepare
14. carefully
15. declare
16. marbles
17. starve
18. margin
19. apartment
20. compare
21. nightmare
22. suitcase
23. meteors
24. celestial
25. astronomy

given.
5. Each animal steps quickly.
6. The circus parade marches noisily.
7. Two tall clowns dance happily.

Page 118
1. government, dangerous, banana, beautiful
2. ocean, again, approve, against, canoe
3. perhaps
4. qualify, cousin
5. season, memory, mosquito, comfort
6. citrus, chorus, industry, surprise

Page 119
1. chorus
2. perhaps
3. dangerous
4. surprise
5. beautiful
6. comfort
7. approve
8. ocean
9. again
10. government
11. banana
12. qualify
13. memory
14. mosquito
15. season
16. cousin
17. citrus
18. against
19. industry

Page 120
Spell correctly: beautiful, season, wonder, ocean, against
Trade places: a/is, the/of
Take out: the (between "the" and "jewel")

Page 121
1. "A Beautiful Memory"
2. Highlights
3. Chicago Tribune
4. The Canoe
5. "Computer Tips for Kids"
6. Industry and the Canadian Government
7. "Stopping by Woods on a Snowy Evening"

Page 122
1. general, animal, final, natural, musical, signal
2. nickel, barrel
3. whistle, simple, pickles, trouble, double, puzzle, tumble, tremble, example, sample, wrinkle, couple

Page 123
1. pickles
2. example
3. signal
4. double
5. puzzle
6. sample
7. whistle
8. musical
9. general
10. natural
11. nickel
12. tumble
13. animal
14. final
15. barrel
16. couple
17. simple
18. trouble
19. tremble

Page 124
Spell correctly: general, puzzle, trouble, whistle, simple
Capitalize: October, Bank, Marvin
Trade places: the/at, things/of

Page 125
1. We tremble excitedly.
2. All of the animals wait obediently.
3. A couple of people busily sell souvenirs.
4. Suddenly the signal is

Page 126
1. teacher, center, toaster, rather, character, whether, discover, answer, another, silver, gather, member, master
2. actor, humor
3. similar, calendar, cellar, polar, sugar

Page 127
1. sugar
2. similar
3. humor
4. silver
5. center
6. another
7. answer
8. character
9. cellar
10. teacher
11. actor
12. master
13. whether
14. polar
15. member
16. toaster
17. discover
18. rather
19. gather

Page 128
Spell correctly: whether, similar, rather, master, center
Capitalize: Hi, My, I
Add period: after "dancer"; after "ballet center"

Page 129
Answers may vary slightly.
1. trying hard to solve something
2. not feeling well; ill
3. immediately
4. to be a model worthy of imitation

Page 130
1. action, inspection, invention, section, election, direction, collection, instruction, fraction, selection, mention
2. information, education, location, nation, vacation, pollution, population, transportation, station

Page 131
1. station
2. vacation
3. population
4. nation
5. fraction
6. mention
7. selection
8. information
9. section
10. transportation
11. invention
12. education
13. collection
14. pollution
15. inspection
16. action
17. instruction
18. location
19. direction

Page 132
Spell correctly: pollution, mention, education, population, action
Capitalize: Mayor, The, The
Take out: in (between "in" and "our"); to (between "to" and "speak")

Page 133
1. 6:30
2. 12:10

3. 2:45
4. 9:05
5. Some of the world's best inventions include the following: the wheel, the gasoline engine, the telephone, and pizza.
6. Three candidates are running for election: Mayor Hibbs, Mrs. Gold, and Mr. Santos.
7. Three topics will be covered on our test: pollution, transportation, and population.

Page 134
1. road, rode, waist, waste, right, write, its, it's, hole, whole, plain, plane, threw, through
2. their, there, they're, to, too, two

Page 135
1. hole
2. road
3. threw
4. its
5. write
6. right
7. too
8. two
9. they're
10. their
11. waist
12. plain
13. it's
14. plane
15. whole
16. through
17. rode
18. to
19. there

Page 136
Spell correctly: their, write, whole, waste, there
Capitalize: Late, Emily, For
Trade places: the/of, our/on

Page 137
1. golf
2. clue
3. destroy
4. earn
5. polite
6. siege
7. pecan
8. easel
9. feud
10. code

Page 138–139
1. beautiful
2. surprise
3. dangerous
4. mosquito
5. ocean
6. against
7. barrel
8. natural
9. couple
10. general
11. example
12. similar
13. humor
14. calendar
15. character
16. whether
17. collection
18. education
19. direction
20. invention
21. they're
22. it's
23. their
24. its
25. there